.

AMY EDMONDSON

Bestselling Author of *The Fearless Organization*

90
DAYS
to
LEVEL
UP

YOUR
TEAMWORK

WILEY

Published by John Wiley & Sons, Inc., Hoboken, New Jersey.
Published simultaneously in Canada.

The manufacturer's authorized representative according to the EU General Product Safety Regulation is Wiley-VCH GmbH, Boschstr. 12, 69469 Weinheim, Germany, e-mail: Product_Safety@wiley.com.

Trademarks: Wiley and the Wiley logo are trademarks or registered trademarks of John Wiley & Sons, Inc. and/or its affiliates in the United States and other countries and may not be used without written permission. All other trademarks are the property of their respective owners. John Wiley & Sons, Inc. is not associated with any product or vendor mentioned in this book.

Limit of Liability/Disclaimer of Warranty: While the publisher and author have used their best efforts in preparing this book, they make no representations or warranties with respect to the accuracy or completeness of the contents of this book and specifically disclaim any implied warranties of merchantability or fitness for a particular purpose. No warranty may be created or extended by sales representatives or written sales materials. The advice and strategies contained herein may not be suitable for your situation. You should consult with a professional where appropriate. Further, readers should be aware that websites listed in this work may have changed or disappeared between when this work was written and when it is read. Neither the publisher nor authors shall be liable for any loss of profit or any other commercial damages, including but not limited to special, incidental, consequential, or other damages.

For general information on our other products and services or for technical support, please contact our Customer Care Department within the United States at (800) 762-2974, outside the United States at (317) 572-3993 or fax (317) 572-4002.

Wiley also publishes its books in a variety of electronic formats. Some content that appears in print may not be available in electronic formats. For more information about Wiley products, visit our web site at www.wiley.com.

Library of Congress Cataloging-in-Publication Data is Available:

ISBN 9781394257959 (Cloth)
ISBN 9781394335527 (ePub)
ISBN 9781394372317 (ePDF)

Cover design: Paul McCarthy

Contents

90-Day Plan

Each week, you'll focus on one element of teamwork that will help you achieve your performance goals. This 90-Day Plan outlines these skills and topics so you can pace yourself, track your progress, and identify the areas that will have the most impact for you. Add your personal goals and vision for success at the bottom of this plan.

Your 90-Day Plan to Level Up Your Teamwork Skills
Performance Goals
• Get ready to learn, innovate, and compete. • Team fearlessly with psychological safety. • Innovate with teaming.
Benchmark Goals
Days 1–30 Get ready to learn, innovate, and compete. Week 1: Understand how teaming is different than teamwork. Week 2: Learn the four pillars of teaming and why they work. Week 3: Lead through teaming. Week 4: Discover how to team across boundaries.

Days 31–60

Team fearlessly with psychological safety.

Week 5: Grasp the power of psychological safety.

Week 6: Make it safe to team.

Week 7: Frame your team for success.

Week 8: Create a fearless organization.

Days 61–90

Innovate with teaming.

Week 9: Aim high.

Week 10: Team up.

Week 11: Fail well.

Week 12: Learn fast.

Personal Goals and Vision for Success

What do you hope to achieve by leveling up?

_____

_____

_____

How could your life change by reaching these goals?

_____

_____

_____

Are you ready to level up? Let's get started!

Introduction

Welcome to *90 Days to Level Up Teamwork*, your guide to taking your leadership skills to the next level in only 90 days. In this guide, I challenge you with actionable, practical goals to build your teamwork skills week by week. You don't have to wait to see results: you'll be learning and growing every week of this 90-Day Plan.

In this guide, I challenge you to do the following:

- Get ready to learn, innovate, and compete.
- Team fearlessly with psychological safety.
- Innovate with teaming.

These overarching performance goals are broken down into benchmark goals for each week: rigorous but achievable targets to let you see immediate progress on your journey.

Each weekly goal comes with insightful readings, engaging activities, and opportunities for self-reflection.

Part I describes the basic activities and conditions that help organizations succeed through teaming, a dynamic kind of teamwork designed to fit the needs of the fast-paced modern workplace. I cover how work gets done, how leaders help make it happen, and how a safe interpersonal environment frees up people to focus on innovation. The model and guidelines presented throughout this part provide readers with a supportive framework for understanding and responding to the dynamics of collective learning. I examine and describe the mindset required to successfully incorporate teaming within an organizational setting and provide a set of leadership practices that can help develop a team-based learning infrastructure.

In Part II, I look at what psychological safety is and why it matters, as well as why it's not the norm in many organizations. I discuss how crucial it is to create an environment where everyone feels free to speak up honestly and mistakes can be admitted without fear. I also talk about what psychological safety *isn't* and why it doesn't mean immunity from consequences. Leaders have a special responsibility to create the conditions of psychological safety, and I discuss what those are. Last, I cover the importance of framing work well and how to actually go about creating a psychologically safe environment.

In Part III, I discuss the four requirements to build a team for innovation: aim high, team up, fail well, and learn fast. Aiming high involves choosing a worthy goal for your team, and I cover what that means and how it spurs innovation. Successful teaming often requires diverse (in many ways) team members, and that diversity brings risks as well as benefits. You will learn how to maximize the benefits and minimize risks. I also explain why "fail well" isn't an oxymoron and the many learning benefits that you can derive from an *intelligent* failure.

In Part I, you will get ready to learn, innovate, and compete with teaming.

In week 1, I define teaming and explain how teaming is different than teamwork. How does it work? What does it take for people to learn how to team? What do people do when teaming? How does teaming produce organizational learning? This week describes the challenges to teaming and shows what it looks like when it's done well. I define teaming and examine why it's so crucial in today's complex organizations.

In week 2, you learn the four pillars of teaming and why they are a must: speaking up, collaboration, experimentation, and reflection. I also look at why those four pillars aren't as easy to achieve as you might think. I review the benefits of teaming and talk about some of the barriers you must overcome to team effectively.

In week 3, I show you how to lead with teaming. My years of research have established four key responsibilities that leaders have to set the stage for successful teaming:

- Frame the situation for learning.
- Make it psychologically safe to team.
- Learn to learn from failure.
- Span occupational and cultural boundaries.

I cover all of these in more depth throughout this 90-Day Plan. In week 3, I also offer strategies for learning from failure.

In week 4, you discover how to team across boundaries. There are many barriers or boundaries to successful teaming. In the modern workplaces, workers are often widely dispersed geographically, have different cultural backgrounds, have varying educational backgrounds, and have widely differing status. But in order to get the results you want, you'll need to overcome these stumbling blocks to successful teaming. In this week, you look at the common types of boundaries, how they interfere with successful teaming, and, most important, how to overcome them.

In Part II, you will discover teaming fearlessly with psychological safety.

In week 5, we begin a deep dive into psychological safety—what it is and why it's important. You will also learn the dangers of an environment where people don't feel psychologically safe. Finally, I explain why psychologically safe high-performing teams only *seem* to make more errors than other teams.

In week 6, you will learn the many benefits of psychological safety. In addition, you will see why it can be so difficult for workers to feel comfortable in speaking up and how interpersonal risk plays into that. I also explain how everyone, but especially leaders, can help encourage psychological safety throughout the organization.

In week 7, you look at the subject of framing and the important responsibilities that leaders have to frame work and the team effectively. Considerable research has shown that when a project is framed well by leadership, successful outcomes are more likely. In this week, you learn what successful framing looks like and strategies for achieving it. I also explain why the "ideal employees" might not be who you think they are.

In week 8, I dive into the hows of psychological safety. How does a leader create a fertile environment for it? One key factor is encouraging employees to use their voice. I examine how to do that and why it matters. You will also read about an interesting case where an employee was fired from Google for expressing an (unpopular) opinion. I examine how it could have been handled differently and how Google could learn from this situation in the future.

In Part III, you will learn how to innovate with teaming by discovering four key concepts to innovation: aim well, team up, fail well, and learn fast.

In week 9, you begin to learn about the first of the key concepts that set the stage for innovation: aiming well. When you are looking to do something that has never been done before, it helps to have a worthy goal. A leader is responsible for not only pointing the team in the direction of an inspiring or meaningful goal but also helping to frame it that way for everyone on the team.

In week 10, I discuss the second key to innovation: teaming up. Contrary to popular belief, some of the most successful teams are composed of strange bedfellows. You will learn about one fascinating real-life example that formed the basis of the movie *Argo*. Diverse skills and backgrounds are often necessary for a successful team, but those differences can create challenges, too. I also cover how to address those boundaries to successful teaming.

In week 11, I cover the third key to innovation: failing well. Despite what you might think, not all failure is created equal. Sometimes, failures can be an essential and productive learning opportunity, but not all failures fall into this category. In this week, I explain the different types of failures and how to make sure that your failures are the right kind. I also cover the responsibilities of a leader in managing failures.

In week 12, I look at the fourth key to innovation: learning fast. When you have those productive failures that you learned about in week 11, it's vital that you learn from them and learn fast. In this week, you discover how to learn fast and how to overcome barriers to it. You will also discover your responsibilities as a leader to prepare your team for learning from its mistakes and setbacks.

If you are ready to level up your teamwork, turn the page and get started!

Performance goal: Get ready to learn, innovate, and compete.

Teaming, coined deliberately to capture the *activity* of working together, presents a new, more flexible way for organizations to carry out interdependent tasks. Unlike the traditional concept of a team, *teaming* is an active process, not a static entity. Imagine a fluid network of interconnected individuals working in temporary teams on improvement, problem-solving, and innovation. Teaming blends relating to people, listening to other points of view, coordinating actions, and making shared decisions.

The following table summarizes the skills you will sharpen over the next 30 days. To keep yourself motivated, consider your personal goals and vision for success. What does teamwork mean to you?

Days 1–30	
Performance Goal: Get ready to learn, innovate, and compete.	
Week 1	**Benchmark Goal: Understand how teaming is different than teamwork.** • What was psychologist Richard Hackman's perspective on teams? • How is teaming different than that traditional understanding? • Do you agree that fear is no longer an effective management strategy in the workplace? • What is the difference between organizing to execute and organizing to learn?
Week 2	**Benchmark Goal: Learn the four pillars of teaming and why they work.** • What are the four pillars of teaming? • What are the benefits of teaming compared to a traditional structured team? • Which of the social and cognitive barriers of teaming have you struggled with in the workplace? • Were you able to handle the barrier effectively? If not, can you think of a better way to handle such a barrier in the future?
Week 3	**Benchmark Goal: Lead through teaming.** • How can leaders promote teaming? • Can you think of a time when you learned a valuable lesson from failure? • Can you recall a failure you should have learned from but didn't?

90 Days to Level Up Your Teamwork

Days 1–30	
Performance Goal: Get ready to learn, innovate, and compete.	
Week 4	**Benchmark Goal: Discover how to team across boundaries.** • What are some of the biggest boundaries or barriers to teaming? • What are some of the challenges of teaming across boundaries of physical distance? • Have you found status a serious boundary in your experience of teamwork?
Personal Goals and Vision for Success	
What do you hope to achieve by leveling up?	
How could your life change by reaching these goals?	

Teaming Is a Verb

Benchmark goal: Understanding how teaming is different than teamwork.

Say the word *team* and the first image that comes to mind is probably a sports team: football players huddled in the mud, basketball players swarming in a full-court press, or baseball players turning a game-saving double play. In sports, great teams consist of individuals who have learned to trust one another. Over time, they have discovered each other's strengths and weaknesses, enabling them to play as a coordinated whole. Similarly, musicians form bands, chamber groups, and orchestras that rely on interdependent talents. A symphony falls apart unless the string section coordinates with the woodwinds, brass, and percussionists. Even when a soloist is featured on stage, the orchestral score has a part for every musician. A successful performance is one in which the musicians complement one another and play in harmony. Like all good teams, they display synergy. The whole is greater than the sum of its parts. The players understand that they succeed or fail together—they win or lose as a team.

In today's complex and volatile business environment, corporations and organizations also win or lose by creating wholes that are greater than the sum of their parts. Intense competition, rampant unpredictability, and a constant need for innovation are giving rise to even greater interdependence and thus demand even greater levels of collaboration and communication than ever before. Teaming is essential to an organization's ability to respond to opportunities and to improve internal processes. Week 1 aims to deepen your understanding of why teaming and the behaviors it requires are so crucial for organizational success in today's environment.

Delving into Teaming

Sports teams and musical groups are both bounded, static collections of individuals. Like most work teams in the past, they are physically located in the same place while practicing or performing together. Members of these teams learn how to interact. They've developed trust and know each other's roles. Advocating stable boundaries, well-designed tasks, and thoughtfully composed membership, many seminal theories of organizational effectiveness explained how to design and manage just these types of static performance teams.

Harvard psychologist Richard Hackman, a preeminent scholar of team effectiveness, established the power of team structures in enabling team performance. According to this influential perspective, well-designed teams are those with clear goals, well-thought-out tasks that are conducive to teamwork, team members with the right skills and experiences for the task, adequate resources, and access to coaching and support. Get the design right, the theory says, and the performance will take care of itself. This model focused on the team as an entity, looking largely within the well-defined bounds of a team to explain its performance. Other research, notably conducted by MIT professor Deborah Ancona, showed that how much a team's members interact with people outside the team boundaries was also an important factor in team performance. Both perspectives worked well in guiding the design and management of effective teams, at least in contexts where managers had the lead time and the run time to invest in composing stable, well-designed teams.

In these prior treatments, *team* is a noun. A team is an established, fixed group of people cooperating in pursuit of a common goal. But what if a team disbands almost as quickly as it was assembled? For example, what if you work in an emergency services facility where the staffing changes every shift, and the team changes completely for every case or client? What if you're a member of a temporary project team formed to solve a unique production problem? Or you're part of a group of managers with a mix of individual and shared responsibilities? How do you create synergy when you lack the advantages offered by the frequent drilling and practice sessions of static performance teams like those in sports and music?

The answer lies in *teaming*.

Teaming is a verb. It is a dynamic activity, not a bounded, static entity. It is largely determined by the mindset and practices of teamwork, not by the design and structures of effective teams. Teaming is teamwork on the fly. It involves coordinating and collaborating without the benefit of stable team structures, because many operations, such as hospitals, power plants, and military installations, require a level of staffing flexibility that makes stable team composition rare. In a growing number of organizations, the constantly shifting nature of work means that many teams disband almost as soon as they've formed. You could be working on one team right now, but in a few days, or even a few minutes, you may be on another team.

Fast-moving work environments need people who know how to team, people who have the skills and the flexibility to act in moments of potential collaboration when and where they appear. They must have the ability to move on, ready for the next such moments. Teaming still relies on old-fashioned teamwork skills such as recognizing and clarifying interdependence, establishing trust, and figuring out how to coordinate. But there usually isn't time to build a foundation of familiarity through the careful sharing of personal history and prior experience, nor is there time for developing shared experiences through practice working together. Instead, people need to develop and use new capabilities for sharing crucial knowledge quickly. They must learn to ask questions clearly and frequently. They must make the small adjustments through which different skills and knowledge are woven together into timely products and services.

Why should managers care about teaming? The answer is simple. Teaming is the engine of organizational learning. By now, everyone knows that organizations need to learn—to thrive in a world of continuous change. But how organizations learn is not as well understood. Organizations are complex entities; many are globally distributed, most encompass multiple areas of expertise, and nearly all engage in a variety of activities. What does it mean for such a complex entity to "learn"? An organization cannot engage in a learning process in any meaningful sense—not in the way an individual can. Yet, when individuals learn, this does not always create change in the ways the organization delivers products and services to customers.

In spite of the obvious need for change, most large enterprises are still managed according to a powerful mindset I call *organizing to execute*.

Organizing to Execute

If you stood on a main street in Detroit around 1900, you would have seen electric trolleys sharing the streets with horse-drawn carriages.

A mere decade later, cars had arrived in force. Though inefficient and unreliable, these increasingly popular cars brought with them the promise of a new, exciting world. For a short time, however, both horse and mechanical horsepower tried to share the streets, sometimes with devastating consequences. Many people found the collision of old and new worlds difficult, especially when those streets became even more crowded with young men from the countryside drawn to the city by the promise of manufacturing jobs.

In this transitional period, it was not obvious to the average worker how much the new industrial era would disrupt the social order by calling for new forms of obedience, unprecedented conformity to routine, and a new mindset that revered systems of control. Self-sufficient farmers and shopkeepers, who had for generations confronted vicissitudes of weather and illness and found ways to survive, would subtly but inexorably be transformed into order followers collecting paychecks from impersonal enterprises.

Organizing to execute found its seminal momentum in Henry Ford's invention of the assembly line: workers focused on fitting cog to component and component to cog. Emphasizing routine procedures, Ford's approach made the working life of employees menial and tedious. Reliable and predictable, Ford's assembly line process was as much a novelty as its product. With the new century, age-old structures for self-reliance were being replaced with the small, repetitive steps that made mass production possible and brought about the modern world of products and services we know today. Ford's success was contingent on a high level of managerial control over employee practices known today as command-and-control management, or top-down management. The practice of top-down management is one component of a broader organizational methodology known as scientific management.

Scientific Management

Ford's intellectual partner as a pioneer in mass production was management expert Frederick Winslow Taylor, who complemented Ford's assembly line with his efficiency methods and scientific measurement. Taylor and his followers devised ways to transform unpredictable and expensive customized work into efficient, economical systems of mass production. Long product life cycles enabled ample payback for the time invested in designing near-foolproof execution systems like the machine-paced assembly line. Periods of stability could be counted on. Products, processes, and even customers were mercifully uniform, minimizing the need for real-time improvisation to respond to unexpected problems, technological changes, or customer needs. Promoting the use of empirical methods, Taylor advocated his model of management and production in two influential monographs, *Shop Management* and *The Principles of Scientific Management.*

As managers today well know, an advantage of these new small, repetitive tasks was their transparency. Small, repetitive tasks are easy to monitor. They make the performance of the individual worker easy to measure. The assumption that firm performance was the cumulative result of thousands and thousands of well-designed and well-executed individual tasks dominated managerial theory and matched the economic reality. Even today, when it comes to issues like efficiency and productivity, most managers and corporate leaders are driven by taken-for-granted beliefs that were first promulgated by Ford and Taylor. For example, many consider the ability to measure and reward the specific, differentiated performance of individuals crucial to good management—a belief that is inaccurate and unhelpful in certain settings.

Ford and Taylor's Legacy

Devotion to efficiency and productivity resulted in two major workplace changes. First, it spurred a demand for professional managers who could oversee a vast complex of work activity. Second, it instilled a basic distrust of the worker. To ensure that workers did their jobs according to specified procedures, objective measurements of individual performance were relatively easy for managers to develop and implement. And, for the most part, workers who tried harder performed better. In mass production settings like the one designed by Ford, opportunities for worker decision-making or creativity were nonexistent. With this transparency, fear worked reasonably well to motivate employees. Whether through a fear of supervisor sanction or loss of material rewards, managers were able to coerce and intimidate workers to ensure high productivity. If there were costs to this approach for the enterprise or corporation, they were not in plain view.

The primary problem this legacy creates for managers today is that these systems produced an overreliance on fear in management practice. As Taylorism gained a foothold in factories across the country, the corporate mood became dour. Taylorism was ruthless. The individual's worth was measured by their contribution to enterprise gains. A history of the United Auto Workers union described factory life in these early days as follows: "Every Ford worker is perfectly aware that he is under constant observation—that he will be admonished if he falls below the fast pace of the department." Even in 1940, decades after the early days of the Ford miracle, a worker could be fired for smiling.

Fear in the Modern Workplace

Unfortunately, draconian management practice is not relegated to the distant past. Consider the rash of employee suicides that brought Foxconn's factory conditions to the public eye in May 2010.

(continued)

(continued)

Said one employee interviewed, "Every day, I repeat the same thing I did yesterday. We get yelled at all the time. It's very tough around here." Reports surfaced of 12-hour standing shifts, having to ask permission to go to the bathroom, and relentless pressure to meet daily manufacturing quotas.

Source: http://www.bloomberg.com/news/2010-06-02/foxconn-workers-in-china-say-meaningless-life-monotony-spark-suicides.html.

Fear and routine have never been limited to blue-collar work. Ford's factory worker can be seen as the precursor to the 1950s' *organization man*, a term coined by sociologist William Whyte. Deindividuating labor was not all that different from deindividuating white-collar work. Much like the assembly line worker, the office-bound organization man was bound by rules, processes, hierarchical structures, and fear. Moreover, the image of the organization man wasn't just promulgated by sociologists. Novelists and writers have portrayed work in large organizations as replete with both monotony and anxiety. American literature has long presented bankers and other managers as organization men, experiencing the same cog-in-the-machine dehumanization as their blue-collar counterparts.

As a society, we are still largely inured to a fear-based work environment. We believe (most of the time, erroneously) that fear increases control. Control reinforces certainty and predictability. We don't immediately see the costs of fear. In fact, many managers believe that without fear people will not work hard enough.

Thriving in the Face of Uncertainty

As customer expectations continue to shift and competition becomes increasingly global, many companies struggle to succeed in a drastically changing landscape. Rapid developments in technology and changes in the legal environment greatly reduce the barriers to entry in a variety of industries, thus introducing new, nimble competitors. Now you see supermarkets, department stores, and funeral homes offering financial services that were formerly the exclusive purview of banks and banking institutions. Likewise, telephone companies offer television service, while television companies offer phone service. Heightened competitive pressure means that even in previously stable industries unexpected changes are occurring in a compressed period of time and creating new, unprecedented challenges.

Consequently, as management and system dynamics expert Peter Senge put it, "The organizations that will truly excel in the future will be the organizations that discover how to tap people's commitment and capacity to learn at all levels in an organization."[1] Learning new skills in an uncertain environment where knowledge is a moving target is now a competitive imperative in most industries. Consider the astonishing expansion of medical knowledge. If you were practicing medicine in 1960, you could subscribe to a few leading professional journals and most likely keep up with the literature in your field. In 1960, there were just 100 articles published on randomized control trials, the gold standard for best practices in medicine. Today more than 10,000 articles reporting on randomized control trials are published annually. An average engineer today sports a wristwatch with more computing power and memory than was available to the team of engineers working in the Apollo program at NASA in the 1960s.

Good-Bye Taylor and Ford . . . Hello Complex Adaptive Systems

The point is that knowledge in fields related to health care, technology, science, and engineering, as well as a host of others, is growing at such a pace that today's workplace is significantly different from that of the industrialized manufacturing era of Ford and Taylor. By now, most leaders and managers recognize that organizations that don't learn are left behind their more innovate and adaptive competitors. In this dynamic environment, successful organizations need to be managed as complex adaptive systems rather than as intricate controlled machines.

The term *complex adaptive system* describes systems that are dynamic and adaptable, much like those found in nature. A system is complex when it has many interacting parts. Feedback loops are a hallmark of complex systems. Feedback loops mean that part A has an impact on part B, which may then affect part C, which feeds back in turn to have an impact on part A. Taken together, these interactions create unpredictable dynamics. Trying to understand, much less predict, what happens in such systems when one is expecting linear, unidirectional relationships—where A influences B, which may influence C, and that is the end of the chain—will produce flawed results.

Complex adaptive systems self-regulate. Not always in preferred ways, mind you, but they change in response to both external and internal triggers. Examples of such systems range from an embryo to an ant colony to a hospital. What these systems have in common is that they encompass a number of similar elements (cells, ants, people) and they self-organize in reaction to external and internal disruptions (often called *perturbations*).

The learning imperative requires relinquishing control as the ultimate goal. It requires embracing the creation of adaptive capabilities as a fundamental organizational competence. It requires flexibility and judgment. It requires a managerial approach that works when organizations face uncertainty created by new technologies, shifting customer preferences, or complex systems. Success requires a shift from organizing to execute to a new way of working that supports collaboration, innovation, and organizational learning.

Learning to Team, Teaming to Learn

Simply put, *teaming* is a way of working that brings people together to generate new ideas, find answers, and solve problems. But people have to learn to team; it doesn't come naturally in most organizations. Teaming is worth learning, because it is essential for improvement, problem-solving, and innovation in a functioning enterprise. The complex interdependencies involved in learning and innovating require the interpersonal skills necessary to negotiate disagreements, overcome technical jargon, and revisit ideas or problems until solutions emerge—all activities supported by teaming. Learning in today's organizations involves what's called *reciprocal interdependence*, where back-and-forth communication and coordination are essential to getting the work done.

Although teaming can help any enterprise improve, it is absolutely critical to success when any of the following conditions are present:

- The work requires people to juggle multiple objectives with minimal oversight.

- People must be able to shift from one situation to another while maintaining high levels of communication and tight coordination. This situation literally defines the practice of teaming.

- It is helpful to integrate perspectives from different disciplines.

- Collaborating takes place across dispersed locations.

- Preplanned coordination is impossible or unrealistic due to the changing nature of the work.

- Complex information must be·processed, synthesized, and put to good use quickly.

Though teaming refers to a dynamic activity rather than to a traditional, bounded group structure, many of its purposes and benefits are grounded in basic principles of teams and teamwork. Among the benefits of teams is their ability to integrate diverse expertise as needed to accomplish many important tasks. Historically, the focus of team research and project implementation was on reorganizing production processes. Increasingly, however, teamwork extends beyond the factory floor.

Using teams to solve problems or shape new strategic directions has been popular in organizations since the early 2000s. In 2003, the Census of Manufacturers from the Manufacturing Performance Institute (MPI) reported that 70 percent of respondents used teams to accomplish their business goals.

Yet all is not perfect with teams and teaming. Despite the fact that team use is steadily increasing, team effectiveness is not keeping up at the same pace. In the previously cited MPI report, only about 14 percent of organizations surveyed rated their teaming efforts as "highly effective," while just over half (50.4 percent) rated their teams as "somewhat effective." Thus, over a third of teams were rated as ineffective. This, in addition to scores of other reports and studies, indicates that although using teams to get interdependent work done can be valuable, achieving the tremendous potential of teams is far more challenging than many expect—and successful teamwork is thus still elusive in many organizations.

Organizing to Learn

Staying competitive, as we have seen, requires learning. Organizing to learn is a way of leading that encourages critical teaming behaviors to promote collective learning. It supports the collaboration needed to solicit employees' knowledge, apply it to new situations or challenges, and to analyze outcomes. Organizing to learn is a way of moving forward in spite of uncertainty. Taking action without certainty can be a daunting prospect in organizations where stability and success are valued over variance and experimentation.

Collective learning includes such activities as collecting, sharing, or analyzing information; obtaining and reflecting on feedback from customers or others; and active experimentation. Individual learning behaviors within a collective learning experience include the following:

- Asking questions
- Sharing information
- Seeking help
- Experimenting with unproven actions
- Talking about mistakes
- Seeking feedback

These learning behaviors enable groups to obtain and process the data needed to adapt and improve. Through collective learning, organizations can detect changes in the environment, learn about customers' requirements, improve members' collective understanding of a situation, or discover the consequences of their previous actions. They require a willingness to take interpersonal risks such as discussing mistakes. This requires leaders who work to create environments that support and encourage sharing, experimenting, and learning.

The old mindset, organizing to execute, has been a century in the making, so it's no wonder that many leaders adopt it by force of habit and training. Organizing to execute has many strengths, especially in its emphasis on discipline and efficiency. However, it also has many risks, particularly when used in highly uncertain or complex contexts.

In these settings, organizing to learn is critical to success. Table 1.1 highlights key differences between the approaches and identifies two distinct mindsets, and the corresponding management practices that leaders can adopt when they are responsible for guiding people and organizations.

Table 1.1   Organizing to Execute Versus Organizing to Learn

Management Approach	Organizing to Execute	Organizing to Learn
Hiring	Conformers, rule followers	Problem-solvers, experimenters
Training	Learn before doing.	Learn from doing.
Measuring performance	Did YOU do it right?	Did WE learn?
Structuring work	Separate expertise	Integrated expertise
Employee discretion allowed	Choose among options.	Experiment through trial and error.
Empowerment means	Employees can deviate from the script if special circumstances make it necessary.	There is no script. Improvise!
Process goal	Drive out variance.	Use variance to analyze and improve.
Watercooler conversation	About the weather	About the work
Business goal	Make money now.	Make money later.
Works when	Path forward is clear.	Path forward is not clear.

Teaming to Learn

The ability to learn is critical for organizations operating in today's fast-paced business environment. Relying on existing knowledge and skills succeeds only if you know exactly what should be done in a job and you expect the process to remain relatively fixed for a significant amount of time. In today's environment, that's the exception, not the rule. In this activity, you delve into teaming and how it works with today's business climate.

Activity

Reflect on the following questions:

How do you define the difference between teaming and teamwork?

_____

_____

_____

What conditions make it necessary to team (as opposed to simply working as a team)?

_____

_____

_____

Do you think teaming is necessary for your organization? If not, do you still think it will be beneficial?

_____

_____

_____

Do you feel fear is a good motivator in the workplace?

_____

_____

_____

Week 2

Identifying the Fundamentals of Teaming

Benchmark goal: Learn the four pillars of teaming and why they work.

Teaming occurs when people apply and combine their expertise to perform complex tasks or develop solutions to novel problems. Often a fluid process, teaming may involve performing with others, disbanding, and joining another group right away. An episode of teaming ends once some or all of the work is complete, but teaming as a mindset—and approach to work—can continue indefinitely. Teaming is normal in the temporary organizations that characterize creative endeavors, such as making a film, or in the coordination of complex events, such as producing a professional conference. In such efforts, a mix of planned and spontaneous coordination often brings multiple players together to team.

Proficient teaming often requires integrating perspectives from a range of disciplines, communicating despite the different mental models that accompany different areas of expertise, and being able to manage the inevitable conflicts that arise when people work together. Fundamentally, this is a matter of developing interpersonal skills related to learning (inquiry, curiosity, listening) and teaching (communicating, connecting, clarifying). Teaming is thus both a mindset that accepts working together actively and a set of behaviors tailored to sharing and synthesizing knowledge. Sometimes teaming requires coordinating across distant locations, which both increases the potential for miscommunication and gives rise to new opportunities for innovation.

Driving Teaming Success

Whether face-to-face or mediated by communication technologies, successful teaming involves these four pillars:

- **Speaking up:** Teaming depends on honest, direct conversation between individuals, including asking questions, seeking feedback, and discussing errors.

- **Collaboration:** Teaming requires a collaborative mindset and behaviors—both within and outside a given unit of teaming—to drive the process.

- **Experimentation:** Teaming involves a tentative, iterative approach to action that recognizes the novelty and uncertainty inherent in every interaction between individuals.

- **Reflection:** Teaming relies on the use of explicit observations, questions, and discussions of processes and outcomes. This must happen on a consistent basis that reflects the rhythm of the work, whether that calls for daily, weekly, or other project-specific timing.

Speaking Up

Candid communication enables teams to incorporate multiple perspectives and tap into individual knowledge. This includes asking questions, seeking feedback, talking about errors, asking for help, offering suggestions, and discussing problems, mistakes, and concerns. Speaking up is particularly crucial when confronting problems or failures of any kind. When people are willing to engage with each other directly and openly, they are better able to make sense of the larger shared work and more likely to generate ideas for improving work processes. Speaking up in this context refers to an interpersonal behavior that enables the development of shared insights from open conversation. It is essential for determining appropriate courses of action in any teaming encounter. Speaking up is also essential for helping people grasp new concepts and methods. Conversing about experiences, insights, and questions builds understanding of new practices and how to perform them. Although many people think of themselves as direct and straightforward, speaking up in the workplace is less common than you might think.

Speaking Up Is Less Common Than You Think

My research with Professor Jim Detert at Cornell University on voice and silence in the workplace shows that speaking up at work is less common than most people think. Through interviews with hundreds of executives, managers, and supervisors in a global high-tech company, we discovered that almost everyone could think of specific instances of not speaking up about a potentially important work-related issue. Most were well-educated, thoughtful people who spanned corporate departments, areas of expertise, and even countries of origin. To explain why people frequently don't speak up, we analyzed hundreds of specific episodes and identified taken-for-granted beliefs about appropriate behavior in hierarchies that are far-reaching in their implications.

(continued)

(continued)

Although most people we studied thought of themselves as pretty straightforward, rather than hesitant or fearful, they still held back potentially important ideas at work. In this study, and several that followed, we showed that there is a remarkable paucity of directness in the workplace. It appears that reluctance to speak up is overdetermined by human nature and by specific realities of the modern economy. From an evolutionary point of view, we're hardwired to overestimate rather than underestimate certain types of risk: it was better for survival to "flee" from threats that weren't really there than to not flee when there was a real risk. And we appear to have inherited emotional and cognitive mechanisms that lead us to avoid perceived risks to our psychological and material well-being. In the workplace, fear of offending people above us in the hierarchy is both natural and widespread, and it means the speaking-up behavior on which teaming depends must be cultivated rather than assumed to be present.

Collaboration

Collaboration is a way of working with colleagues that is characterized by cooperation, mutual respect, and shared goals. It involves sharing information, coordinating actions, discussing what's working and what's not, and perpetually seeking input and feedback. Teaming depends on collaborative behaviors within and between departments or organizations. Clearly, without collaboration, teaming easily breaks down. Plans are less well informed, and the execution of plans suffers from poor coordination. A collaborative attitude is also essential to shared reflection that may occur following coordinated action, because it enables full and thoughtful sharing of expertise and promotes the development of broader and deeper lessons from any experience. Imagine a product development team that doesn't collaborate with the marketing group and thereby fails to incorporate vital customer preferences or feedback!

Experimentation

Experimentation means expecting not to be right the first time. Borrowed from the experiments of scientists, experimentation behavior is a way of acting that centrally involves learning from the results of action. In teaming, experimentation behavior involves reaching out to others to assess the impact of one's actions on them, and also testing the implications of one's ideas with respect to what others are thinking. Experimentation is a vital aspect of teaming because of the uncertainty inherent in interdependent action. It's also a crucial part of learning.

Reflection

Reflection is the habit of critically examining the results of actions to assess results and uncover new ideas. Some teams engage in reflection on a daily basis. Others reflect at a natural break in the project, such as at halftime for sports teams, or when documenting aspects of a patient's care in a chart after a medical visit. Project teams may explicitly engage in a reflection exercise only when a project is completed. The after-action reviews conducted by the US Army following military exercises are explicit reflection sessions that use a rigorous structured approach to assess what occurred against what was planned or expected. Reflection does not necessarily mean extensive sessions to thoroughly analyze team process or performance, but rather is often quick and pragmatic. Reflection in action, for example, is the critical, real-time examination of a process so it can be adjusted based on new knowledge or, more often, in response to subtle feedback received from the work itself. Reflection as a basis for effective teaming is more a behavioral tendency than a formal process. In one study of surgical teams, for example, I found no differences in outcomes for teams with formal reflection sessions compared to those without such sessions; the teams that succeeded were those that were constantly reflecting aloud on what they were observing and thinking, as a way of figuring out how to work together more effectively. For some types of teams, however, it may be more appropriate to wait for outcomes to be available before stopping to reflect on team process, in which case a more structured approach, such as a formal project review, is extremely valuable.

These four behaviors are the pillars of effective teaming. The challenges encountered on the factory floor, in the operating room, and around the glass-topped tables in corporate conference rooms differ significantly in look and feel, as well as in the nature of the work. Yet speaking up, collaboration, experimentation, and reflection are crucial behaviors across these disparate settings. In all of them, leaders who themselves embrace these behaviors make it easier for others to act in ways that support teaming. In addition to these behavioral tendencies, however, leaders must also understand the cyclical, recursive nature of the actual teaming process.

The Benefits of Teaming

One of the most successful product launches in history, Motorola's 2004 RAZR mobile phone, was the result of successful teaming. Battling fierce global competition in the mobile phone market in 2003, Motorola set out to create the thinnest phone ever released. Electrical engineer Roger Jellicoe was chosen to lead the team. In addition to designing the thinnest phone ever, Jellicoe's instructions were to create a thing of beauty, a device more like jewelry than a mere utilitarian object. To partner in leading the project, he chose mechanical engineer Gary Weiss, with whom he knew he could work well. Twenty Motorola engineers were invited to join the teaming effort with its ambitious deadline. They came from different groups and locations to collaborate in an otherwise unremarkable facility an hour from Chicago.

Speaking up and experimentation were critical to their success. Neither ideas nor criticisms were held back, as perpetual experimentation and debate led to possibilities and prototypes that were attempted, rejected, altered, tweaked, and refined. A core challenge was the integration of style and technology. Numerous trade-offs, mostly between appearance and functionality, were considered, and the team resisted easy compromises, pushing instead for elegant solutions to the tough problems they confronted. By experimenting with different configurations, the team hit on the idea of putting the battery next to the circuit board (prior phones had them stacked) to reduce thickness. It worked, allowing the ultra-thin design that gave the phone its appeal and its name.

The team's innovative solution ignored existing human factors experts who had strong views about how wide a cell phone could be to feel right in a person's hand. Experimenting with a wider mock-up of the phone, the team decided the experts were wrong. Reflection was built into the teaming process from the beginning. Meeting every afternoon at 4:00 p.m., the group discussed the day's progress, and reported on the status of such components as the antenna, speaker, keypad, or light source. Scheduled for an hour, the meetings frequently ran past 7:00 p.m. These meetings were a primary mechanism for the team's focused conversation and debate. Reporting on failures as easily as successes and breakthroughs, everyone was engaged in the process of offering ideas and criticisms.

The project's biggest setback occurred when it missed its ambitious initial deadline, but the result, only a few months later and still within a fast time line, was worth waiting for: Motorola unveiled the RAZR, the thinnest phone ever produced, before the end of 2004, and went on to sell 50 million RAZR mobile phones within the next two years and 110 million over four years.

Performance

Whether a new product development team made up of designers, marketers, and engineers, or a cardiac surgery team made up of surgeons, nurses, perfusionists, and anesthesiologists, the benefits of teaming for organizational learning and performance are significant. In particular, teaming helps organizations develop new routines and implement new technologies to meet the demands of a changing context. These kinds of organizational changes call for teaming because they require understanding and coordination across departments and disciplines. Teams are an organization's best change agents. Most models of change management call for a change leadership team or a change implementation team to promote better ideas and greater buy-in. But it shouldn't stop there. What really matters is not just the creation of a team, but how those selected work with each other and with other members of the organization to help create change in a dynamic, learning-oriented way. These change agents must listen, coordinate, and continually make adjustments in plans to accommodate each other's input. This naturally gives rise to uncertainty and requires attention and sensitivity to feedback. The core behaviors of teaming thus drive organizational performance by facilitating the creation of new knowledge, new processes, and new products. Performance improves when new knowledge is put to good use, also enabled by teaming.

Engaged Employees

Teaming has a positive effect on people's experience at work. Interacting directly with people who have different knowledge and skills makes work more interesting, enriching, and meaningful. In organizations where teaming is common, employees learn from each other, enjoy a broader understanding of the work and how it gets done from start to finish, and can better see and act on opportunities for improvement. For example, Simmons Mattress Company introduced team training to raise employee technical and interpersonal skills, which in turn led to greatly increased awareness of the contributions of other employees working in different parts of the manufacturing process. Once everyone began to understand what unseen colleagues did all day, why it was difficult, and how the combined tasks came together to make an entire mattress, not to mention an entire sales and distribution operation, they enjoyed the work more, and were also more productive.

Social and Cognitive Barriers to Teaming

I've spent an inordinate amount of time studying people in hospitals. People working in hospitals face some particularly challenging work environments. Demands for coordination are great, time is tight, and the stakes are high. As a result, the rest of us can learn a lot from understanding how the best hospitals manage these inherent challenges effectively. Medical knowledge and best care practices, which are vast and constantly updated, must be consulted to inform high-stakes, cross-disciplinary communication and action, often under immense time pressure. And, unfortunately, even in a hospital—a setting that calls for nearly constant teaming—cooperation and trust face many challenges.

Serious Work Means Serious Tension

As Wynton Marsalis, artistic director for Jazz at Lincoln Center, says of his work with other jazz musicians, "There are always tensions that come up. Part of working is dealing with tensions. If there's no tension, then you're not serious about what you're doing."

Certainly, teaming sometimes goes well in today's organizations. People recognize their interdependence and work effectively together. They offer their ideas freely, carrying out their part of the collective work and responding thoughtfully to others' ideas and actions. At other times, however, teaming breaks down and coordination fails. Signals get crossed or conflicting opinions derail the conversation. Many teaming efforts—whether in routine, complex, or innovation operations—start with high hopes, only to falter. What are some of the obstacles to effective teaming?

People Don't Always Get Along

Teaming requires participants to productively manage the inevitable conflicts that arise when people work together in serious endeavors. Well-functioning teams are powerful, but rarely static. They are as hard to create as to sustain. Many tasks are technically complex to begin with and present interdependencies that make them even more so. Personality, leadership, resource allocation, differences in knowledge and background—any problems encountered in these areas can give rise to misunderstanding or dysfunction. Fear is a major barrier to teaming. Similarly, lacking a clear, shared objective also inhibits the effortful behaviors that comprise teaming. Organizational factors, such as bureaucracy, layers of management, or contradictory incentive systems, also get in the way. Teaming is as difficult as it is necessary.

It's far easier for an individual to have a clear and well-bounded task to do over and over again than to figure out how to carry out more complex and interdependent work with others. Interdependent work requires coordination through back-and-forth communication to do it well. When we are interdependent, it necessarily means we cannot do everything that must be done alone. This is a rather humbling realization, and many shy away from embracing it. It can be hard for people to muster both the humility and the genuine curiosity that is needed to really learn from others. It turns out that cognitive, interpersonal, and organizational factors all get in the way of effective learning in teams. It's a cruel irony—our success depends on effective collaboration and learning, the essence of teaming, but these don't come naturally either for individuals or the social systems we create. The following sections examine the cognitive and structural factors that inhibit teaming.

Silence Is Easier Than Speaking Up

When leaders fall into a default "do-it-my-way" management style, it silences nearly everyone except the person with the loudest voice or the largest office. But silence in today's economic environment is deadly. Silence means good ideas and possibilities don't bubble up, and problems don't get addressed. Silence stymies teaming. Most people feel a need to manage what I call interpersonal risk—a risk that others will think less of them—so as to minimize harm to their image, especially in the workplace, and especially in the presence of bosses and others who hold formal power. One way to minimize risk to one's image is simply to avoid speaking up unless you're sure you're right, avoid admitting mistakes, and, of course, never ask questions or raise tentative ideas that you're not sure have merit. Although this approach may work for individuals—protecting them from being seen by others in an unfavorable light—it is clearly problematic for organizations and their customers.

Shhhh, Here Comes the Boss

Research shows that hierarchy, by its very nature, dramatically reduces speaking up by those lower in the pecking order. We are hardwired, and then socialized, to be acutely sensitive to power, and to work to avoid being seen as deficient in any way by those in power. Most of this behavior is unconscious. As a result, in most organizations, even if leaders at the top of the hierarchy say they welcome employee feedback, and even if people have the knowledge and training to say something of importance, they still may remain silent out of fear of negative consequences.

Research does show, however, that leaders can promote speaking up through particular behaviors and actions. Most important, when leaders explicitly communicate that they respect employees, it makes it easier for employees to volunteer their knowledge. More specifically, by acknowledging the need for the knowledge and skills that others bring, leaders issue a credible invitation for people to speak up. Mistakes, in particular, require active encouragement if they are to be reported or discussed. In sum, speaking up is not natural in organizations, but it can and does happen, particularly when leaders actively model, invite, and reward candor and openness. By contrast, inaccessibility or a failure to acknowledge vulnerability can contribute to a reluctance to incur the interpersonal risks of teaming behavior.

Disagreement

Speaking up brings challenges, too. As soon as people speak up and communicate freely with one another, there is bound to be disagreement and sometimes seemingly irresolvable conflict. The problem with disagreement is not that it occurs; the problem is the sense-making in which people spontaneously engage when disagreement occurs. All of us have at one point or another spontaneously attributed unflattering motives, traits, or abilities to those who disagree with our strongly held view. In such cases, we might say something like "She doesn't get it" or "He's just out for himself."

Naïve Realism

We are all prone to *naïve realism*, a term coined by psychologist Lee Ross (1977), which is a person's "unshakable conviction that he or she is somehow privy to an invariant, knowable, objective reality—a reality that others will also perceive faithfully, provided that they are reasonable and rational."[1] So, when others misperceive our "reality," we conclude that it must be because they are unreasonable or irrational and "view the world through a prism of self-interest, ideological bias, or personal perversity." And therein lies the trouble.

One outcome of naïve realism is that people tend to see their own views as more common than they really are, leading them to falsely assume that others share their views. For example, someone might say, "We need to dramatically curb carbon emissions to prevent further global warming." Or, "Everyone knows we have the best medical system in the world." Social psychologists call this the *false consensus effect*. And such assumptions usually go unnoticed—until unexpectedly refuted when someone disagrees. This means, if someone replies, "I don't think human activity is contributing to climate change. Temperature fluctuations have gone on for millennia," the original speaker may spontaneously conclude that the responder is closed-minded, wrong-headed, or worse. Similarly, someone might respond to the second statement, "If we have the best medical care, why do we rank 36th in the world for life expectancy?" while privately viewing the original speaker as ignorant or misguided. For most people, finding out that a friend or colleague disagrees with us on something we care about is usually an unpleasant surprise.

The Fundamental Attribution Error

The second cognitive error that makes it hard to cope with conflict productively was dubbed the *fundamental attribution error* by Lee Ross. The term describes our failure to recognize situational causes of events and our tendency instead to overattribute individuals' personality or ability as likely causes. An outgrowth of this cognitive error is that we tend to explain others' shortcomings as related to their ability or attitude, rather than to the circumstances they face. That is, we blame the people for things that go wrong—not the situation. Every parent of more than one child has heard, "Don't blame me, it's his fault." In the workplace, the same thing happens, even if the words are less direct and unambiguous.

It's almost amusing to realize that we do exactly the opposite in explaining our own failures. That is, we spontaneously attribute them to external factors. For example, if we show up late for a meeting, we may blame circumstances outside our control, like rush-hour traffic. If a subordinate is late for a meeting, however, we think he is not committed to the project, or that he's disorganized. On both sides of the attribution coin, we make judgments effortlessly—remaining largely unaware that there was an alternative cause to consider. As natural and sometimes humorous as this asymmetry is, it creates a couple of problems for teaming. First, when we blame others for things that go wrong, productive discussion of the issues is less likely to occur. Worse, we tend to believe we have sized up the situation and its causes accurately. Second, we begin to think less of others, and then may be less motivated to engage wholeheartedly in teaming with them.

Tension and Conflict

The fundamental problem with disagreements, and the cognitive structures that exacerbate them, is that they create tensions in a group. Tensions are to be expected when teaming. Although rarely fun, tensions are not always bad. They can evoke creativity, sharpen ideas, and refine analyses. But there's a catch: patience, wisdom, and skill are needed to transform tensions into positive results. This is because most of us naturally resist tensions and the conflict they invariably bring.

Teaming to Learn

Teaming in organization can often be successful, but it can often be stymied by various barriers. In this activity, spend some time thinking about your own career and the barriers to teaming that you've encountered.

Activity

Reflect on the following questions:

Can you think of a time when you were guilty of naïve realism? How do you think you can safeguard against this in the future?

_____

_____

_____

Of the major barriers to teaming, which seems most insurmountable to you?

_____

_____

_____

Can you think of a time when interpersonal conflict got in the way of a team working effectively? Did the team handle it well? If not, what could they have done differently?

_____

_____

_____

Identifying the Fundamentals of Teaming

Supporting Teaming as a Leader

Benchmark goal: Lead through teaming.

Teaming and learning do not happen automatically. Instead, they require coordination and some structure to ensure that insights are gained from members' collective experience and used to guide subsequent action. As research demonstrates across varied cases and settings, teaming and learning both depend on the deliberate exercise of leadership. It takes leadership to understand and resolve conflict and to instigate thoughtful conversations about errors. It takes leadership to adhere to process discipline and to help people remember to explore and experiment. In short, leadership is needed to help groups build shared understanding and coordinate action.

In nearly two decades of research, I've discovered that leaders have four main responsibilities to set the stage for successful teaming:

- Frame the situation for learning.

- Make it psychologically safe to team.

- Learn to learn from failure.

- Span occupational and cultural boundaries.

These four actions are not solely practices intended for teaming and learning. In fact, these individual practices translate directly to improved leadership and performance under nearly any circumstance. Taken together, however, they form the foundation for leading a successful teaming effort and provide a path forward for integrating learning into everyday execution.

In addition, leaders play a key role in making sure that the team learns from those (inevitable) failures. This week, you focus on the special responsibility that a leader has to support successful teaming.

Frame the Situation for Learning

Framing is crucial for leading the kind of change necessary to engage people as active learners. Leaders seeking to facilitate teaming and produce organizational learning must frame their project in a way that motivates others to collaborate. Researchers agree, however, that many of our spontaneous frames at work are inherently about self-protection. These self-protective frames dramatically inhibit opportunities to collaborate, learn, and improve. However, people can learn to reframe and shift from spontaneous, self-protective frames to reflective, learning-oriented frames. Doing so involves interdependent team leaders, empowered teams, and an aspirational purpose.

Make It Psychologically Safe to Team

An environment of psychological safety is an essential element of organizations that succeed in today's complex and uncertain world. The term *psychological safety* describes a climate in which people feel free to express relevant thoughts and feelings without fear of being penalized. Although it sounds simple, the ability to ask questions, seek help, and tolerate mistakes while colleagues watch can be unexpectedly difficult. Because coordinating and integrating complex tasks requires people to ask questions, share thoughts openly, and act without excessive concern about what others think of them, teaming flourishes with psychological safety and diminishes without it.

Learn to Learn from Failure

An essential, if difficult, teaming activity is learning from failure. Failure, broadly defined, encompasses both the small and large events in organizations that don't go as planned. Examples include a defect occurring in an assembly process, a new drug failing in clinical trials, or a strategy meeting breaking down. Learning from failures of all kinds is as vital as it is difficult. No one wants to look bad in front of their peers, and few of us want to admit failure. Yet failure is a necessary aspect of both teaming and organizational learning. Failures of many kinds offer the chance to gain new insights into how to improve a process or product. The secret for organizations is to figure out how to gather and act on, rather than ignore or suppress, this potentially valuable information.

Span Occupational and Cultural Boundaries

Teams that succeed today don't merely work well around a shared conference table; they also have the ability to collaborate across boundaries and reach people who have the knowledge and information to help them apply resources effectively. Rapid developments in technology and the greater emphasis on globalization have dramatically increased the significance of boundary spanning in today's work environment. The information technology that has enabled us to communicate instantaneously across continents, however, sometimes leaves us with a false sense of confidence that productive teamwork is merely a click away. Education and other socializing processes lead people to favor their own group, discipline, location, or department. Ignoring such boundaries can easily blindside even the most well-intentioned teaming efforts.

Leading Through Failure

Teaming rarely unfolds perfectly, without any bumps, glitches, or failures. This means that the ability to learn from failure is an essential teaming skill. And although most leaders say they understand the importance of failure to the learning process, not many truly embrace it. In my research, I've found that even companies that have invested significant money and effort into becoming learning organizations struggle when it comes to the day-to-day mindset and activities of learning from failure. Managers in these companies were highly motivated to help their organizations learn in order to avoid recurring failures and mistakes. In some cases, they and their teams had devoted many hours to after-action reviews and post-mortems. Even these types of painstaking efforts fall short, however, if managers or leaders think about failure the wrong way.

Most leaders I've talked to believe that failure is bad. They also believe that if failure does occur, learning from it is pretty straightforward: simply ask people to reflect on what they did wrong and instruct them to avoid similar actions in the future. Or, better yet, assign a team to review what happened and develop a report to distribute. Unfortunately, these widely held beliefs are misguided. Here's the simple truth about failure: it is sometimes bad, sometimes good, and often inevitable. Good, bad, inevitable—learning from organizational failures is anything but straightforward.

To learn from mistakes and missteps, organizations must employ new and better ways to go beyond lessons that are superficial (procedures weren't followed) or self-serving (the market just wasn't ready for our great new product). This requires jettisoning old cultural beliefs and stereotypical notions of success and replacing them with a new paradigm that recognizes that some failures are inevitable in today's complex work organizations and that successful organizations will be those that catch, correct, and learn from failures quickly.

Developing a Learning Approach to Failure

Because psychological and organizational factors inhibit both failure identification and analysis, a fundamental reorientation is needed to successfully learn from failure. Individuals and groups must be motivated to embrace the difficult and often emotionally challenging lessons that failures reveal. Doing so requires a spirit of curiosity and openness, as well as exceptional patience and a tolerance for ambiguity. These traits and behaviors are best characterized by what, in the management literature, has been termed an *inquiry orientation*. This type of orientation is presented as a contrast to an *advocacy orientation*. Both terms describe contrasting communication behaviors and distinct approaches to group decision-making.

Advocacy and Inquiry Orientations

Organizational structures and processes can hinder the ability of a group to learn from failure. In groups characterized by an advocacy orientation, these structures and processes support a top-down management approach and the organizational status quo. Therefore, when trying to incorporate the unique knowledge of different members, the unintentional results often include antagonism, a lack of listening and learning, and limited psychological safety for challenging authority.

An inquiry orientation is characterized by the perception among group members that multiple alternatives exist and that frequent dissent is necessary. These perceptions result in a deeper understanding of issues, the development of new possibilities, and an awareness of others' reasoning. This orientation can counteract common group tensions and process failures. Learning about the perspectives, ideas, and experiences of others when facing uncertainty and high-stakes decisions is critical to making appropriate choices and finding solutions to novel problems. But how can leaders promote an inquiry orientation to facilitate learning? The terms *exploratory response* and *confirmatory response* have recently been used to describe distinct ways that leaders can orient individuals and groups to respond to potential failures.

Confirmatory and Exploratory Responses

Leaders play an important role in determining a group's orientation to a perceived failure. Facing small or ambiguous problems, leaders can respond in one of two basic ways: confirmatory or exploratory responses. A confirmatory response by leaders reinforces accepted assumptions, naturally triggering an advocacy orientation. When individuals seek information in this mode, they look for data that confirms existing beliefs, which is a natural human response. Leaders encourage or reinforce a confirmatory response, when they act in ways consistent with established frames and beliefs. This often means they're passive or reactionary rather than active and forward-looking.

In uncertain, risky, or novel situations, an exploratory response is more appropriate. Rather than supporting existing assumptions, an exploratory response requires a deliberate shift in the mindset of a leader. This alters the way a leader interprets and diagnoses the situation at hand. This shift involves challenging and testing existing assumptions and experimenting with new behaviors and possibilities. When leaders adopt an exploratory approach, they embrace ambiguity and openly acknowledge gaps in knowledge. They recognize that their current understanding may require revision, and so they actively search for evidence in support of alternative hypotheses. Rather than seeking to prove what they already believe, exploratory leadership encourages inquiry and experimentation. This deliberate response helps to accelerate learning through proactive information gathering and simple, rapid experimentation.

It would be nice if transforming an organization into a learning enterprise was just a matter of altering the orientation and perspective of a single leader. But of course it's not that simple. A productive approach to failure requires leadership, exercised by many individuals, to cultivate diagnostic acumen. In this way, an organizational culture of curiosity and analysis can be developed and nurtured. This helps people to develop a clearheaded understanding of what happened, rather than just identifying "who did it" when something goes wrong. Doing this well means insisting on consistent reporting of failures, encouraging deep and systematic analysis, and promoting the proactive search for opportunities to experiment.

Strategies for Learning from Failures

Failure tolerance is a smart strategy for any organization wishing to gain new knowledge. Because organizations are more and more likely to encompass complex work and face unpredictable environments, a growing number of failures are of the complex type, and it's crucial to anticipate and respond to them quickly. Moreover, great strategic advantage can be gained from intelligent failures. But neither type of failure can be put to good use without a rational approach to diagnosis and discussion. Given that failure is inherently emotionally charged, responding to it requires specific, purposeful strategies. Three activities—detection, analysis, and experimentation—are critical to learning from failures. As Table 3.1 shows, these three activities apply to all types of failures, although how they're carried out varies in important ways.

Table 3.1 Strategies for Learning from Failure

	Detect Failure	Analyze Failure	Promote Failure
Strategies for learning from preventable failures	Make it safe for employees to check with managers and peers when unsure what to do. Reward problem detection. Reward false alarms (potential failures that turn out fine) for their value in learning and practicing.	Develop and employ classic techniques for process improvement.	Encourage small tests to ensure process viability, especially in the face of gradual changes in technology or customer preferences.

Table 3.1 *(continued)*

	Detect Failure	Analyze Failure	Promote Failure
Strategies for learning from complex failures	Make it safe to report errors and problems. Reward finding system vulnerabilities. Reward rapid reporting of small and large failures.	Convene cross-functional groups to identify what happened from multiple perspectives.	Encourage offline tests to identify new failure modes so as to add new fail-safe mechanisms into processes.
Strategies for learning from intelligent failures	Make it safe to experiment. Reward early detection of failed experiments. Reward early declaration of failed projects.	Employ scientific method to analyze data systematically. Avoid superficial insights from quick assessment of trends or patterns. Include multiple perspectives.	Experiment more often, with more variety. Conduct pilots as experiments to identify failure modes rather than as demonstrations of success.

Supporting Teaming as a Leader

Failure Detection: Support Systems for Identifying Failure

The first crucial strategy to master is the proactive and timely identification of failure. This is especially true of the type of small and seemingly inconsequential failures that lead to large, often catastrophic, failures. Any organization can detect big, expensive failures. It's the little ones that often go unnoticed. In many organizations, any failure that can be hidden is hidden, so long as it's unlikely to cause immediate or obvious harm. Even more common is the tendency to withhold bad news related to pending failures as long as humanly possible.

Recognizing this, Allan Mulally, soon after being hired as CEO of Ford Motors, created a new system for identifying failures. Understanding how difficult it is for early-stage failures to make it up the corporate hierarchy, he asked his managers to color code their reports: green for good, yellow for caution, red for problems. Mulally was frustrated when, during the first couple of meetings, managers coded most of their operations green. He reminded managers how much money the company had recently lost and asked pointedly whether everything was indeed going along well. It took this prodding for someone to speak up, tentatively offering a first yellow report. After a moment of shocked silence in the group Mulally clapped, and the tension was broken. After that, yellow and red reports came in regularly.

Ford's is not an isolated story. In companies around the world, even the most senior executives can be reluctant to convey bad news to bosses and colleagues. Shooting the messenger remains an enduring and problematic phenomenon, so it's essential for leaders to proactively create conditions in which messages of failure travel up and across an organizational hierarchy. To do this, leaders need to engage in three essential activities: embrace the messenger, gather data and solicit feedback, and reward failure detection.

Embrace the Messenger

Savvy managers understand the risks of unbridled toughness. An overly punitive response to an employee mistake may be more effective in stifling information about problems than in making your organization better. This is obviously not a good result. Managers' ability to quickly diagnose and resolve problems depends on their ability to learn about them. Organizations with a habit of punishing mistakes or errors will discourage this process. This means that psychological safety (Part II of this 90-Day Plan) is the bedrock of any genuine failure identification and analysis effort.

Gather Data and Solicit Feedback

My research has found that a lack of access to data on failures is the most important barrier to managers learning from them. This is especially true for preventable and complex failures. In these circumstances, people often believe that no failures are acceptable, so hiding them can seem the only feasible approach. That inaccessibility can be due as much to human resistance to identifying failure as to technical difficulties in understanding small mistakes. To overcome this barrier, organizational leaders must develop systems, procedures, and cultures that proactively identify failure.

Soliciting feedback is an effective way of gathering data and surfacing many types of failures. Feedback from customers, employees, and other sources can expose failures such as communication breakdowns, the inability to meet goals, or a lack of customer satisfaction. Proactively seeking feedback from customers often helps manufacturers and service providers identify and address failures in a timely manner. If you believe identifying customer dissatisfaction is a luxury, bear in mind that only 5–10 percent of dissatisfied customers choose to complain following a service failure. Instead, most simply switch providers. This means that if service companies fail to learn from their failures, they're guaranteed to lose customers.

Reward Failure Detection

Failures must be exposed as early as possible to enable learning in an efficient and cost-effective way. This requires a proactive effort on the part of managers to surface available data on failures and use it in a way that promotes learning. The detection challenge for intelligent failures lies in knowing when to declare defeat in an experimental course of action. The human tendency to hope for the best impedes early failure identification and is often exacerbated by strict organizational hierarchies. As a result, fruitless research projects are frequently kept going much longer than is scientifically rational or economically prudent. We throw good money after bad, hoping to pull a rabbit out of a hat. In innovation operations, this happens more often than most managers realize. Engineers' or scientists' intuition can be telling them for weeks that a project has fatal flaws, but making the formal decision to call it a failure may be delayed for months. Considerable resources are saved when such projects are stopped in a timely way and people are freed up to explore the next potential innovation.

Teaming as a Leader

Leaders have a special responsibility to encourage teaming. In this activity, you will examine the leader's role in encouraging teaming.

Activity

Reflect on the following questions:

Of a leader's four main responsibilities to promote teaming, which do you think is most important?

_____

_____

_____

Do you agree that many of our spontaneous frames are self-protective? Why or why not?

_____

_____

_____

Can you think of a failure you learned from? Describe the failure and what you learned from it. Do you think that failure was inevitable?

_____

_____

_____

Week 4

Breaking Through Barriers

Benchmark goal: Discover how to team across boundaries.

When teaming across boundaries works, the results can be awe-inspiring. Managing a complex rescue operation, launching a space shuttle, producing a big-budget movie, or delivering a large engineering and construction project are all examples of complex uncertain work that requires multiple areas of expertise, and even multiple organizations, for its completion. The problem is that all too often teaming is thwarted by communication failures that take place at the boundaries between professions, organizations, and other groups. People think they're communicating, they participate in endless meetings, and they work hard, only to have their projects fail. Why? As individuals bring diverse expertise, skills, perspectives, and goals together in unique team configurations to accomplish challenging goals, they must overcome the hidden challenge of communicating across multiple types of boundaries. Some boundaries are obvious—like 2,000 feet of rock, or being in different countries with different time zones. Others are subtle, such as when two engineers working for the same company in different facilities unknowingly bring different taken-for-granted assumptions about how to carry out a particular technical procedure to a collaboration.

This week, I describe the boundaries that team members frequently must cross while working together on complex problems. After examining why boundaries matter, I describe three types of boundaries that confront teaming in today's global organizations. I then provide guidelines for successfully teaming across boundaries to create possibilities for organizational learning.

Visible and Invisible Boundaries

Boundaries refer to the divisions between identity groups. An identity group exists for any meaningful category in which a person belongs, such as gender, occupation, or nationality. Some identity groups, and their corresponding boundaries, are more visible than others. Gender, for example, is visible. Occupation is less visible—except when clothing gives it away. What is invisible, however, are the taken-for-granted assumptions and mindsets that people hold in different groups. For teaming to be successful, managers and team members must be aware that they come together with different perspectives, often taking for granted the "rightness" of their own beliefs and values. This means it's not enough to simply say, let's band together and it will all work out. No matter how much goodwill may be involved, boundaries limit collaboration in ways that are often invisible but nonetheless powerful.

Taken-for-Granted Assumptions

Processes of education, licensing, hiring, and socializing contribute to beliefs that lead people to favor their own group or location, and to unconsciously view the knowledge of their own group as especially important. It's as if there's a wall that separates engineers from marketers, nurses from doctors, and designers in Beijing from designers in Boston. Most people take knowledge that lies on their side of a boundary for granted, making it hard to communicate with those on the other side. Paraphrasing an observation once made by communications theorist Marshall McLuhan, we don't know who discovered water, but it wasn't the fish. In other words, the context in which we work, day in and day out, is often invisible to us. Presumably, fish don't think much about water; they take it for granted.

Communication with anyone from a different group, whether the difference is demographic or organizational, is fraught with small hurdles. Teams within organizations often must coordinate objectives, schedules, or resources with other teams, departments, or locations. This requires discovering and revealing taken-for-granted assumptions to avoid misunderstanding and error. But by their very nature, taken-for-granted assumptions are notoriously hard to recognize, so it helps to be aware that they exist and to be on the lookout for them.

Specialization and Globalization

Two related trends have increased the need for teaming across boundaries. First, knowledge and expertise evolve ever more rapidly. In most fields, the rate of new knowledge development requires people to invest considerable time just to stay current in their own area of expertise. Especially in technical fields, the explosion of new knowledge leads inexorably to greater specialization. Fields spawn new subfields, and new subfields spawn even more specialized subfields. For example, electrical engineering, once a subfield of physics, became its own discipline by 1900, and today splits into the several distinct subfields of power systems, signal processing, and computer architecture. More generally, technical knowledge and specialized jargon proliferate, making it difficult to keep up with other, even closely related, fields of inquiry. Highly specialized professionals thus find themselves needing to collaborate to carry out the important work of the organization, whether developing a new cell phone or caring for a cancer patient.

Second, global competition has led to ever more compressed time frames: product life cycles are shrinking, lead times for getting new products to market are shorter, and scientific researchers face more threats of being scooped in their work by a lab halfway around the world. Time pressures mean that a structured approach, in which managers plan each aspect of a large development project with specialized tasks to be accomplished separately in carefully structured phases, are unrealistic. This planning becomes even less realistic when completed tasks are "thrown over the wall" to other functions or disciplines. Instead, the walls between disciplines have come down, and simultaneous work on related tasks must be coordinated and negotiated in a dynamic teaming journey.

Individuals or departments cannot accomplish meaningful results in isolation. The chances of individual components, developed separately, coming together into meaningful, functional wholes—new product, feature film, or rescue operation—without intense communication across the boundaries are exceedingly low. Considering these two factors—increasing specialization and global competition—there are numerous benefits to learning how to transcend boundaries that exist between people, departments, or specialties. Understanding how to break down these walls includes developing a deeper understanding of the varieties of diversity and how they relate to the boundaries that exist both within and between work groups.

Three Types of Boundaries

Diversity is an important topic in research on teams and teaming, yet researchers lack consensus on a single clear definition of diversity.

Katherine Klein and Dave Harrison, professors at Wharton and Penn State, respectively, defined diversity as "the distribution of differences among the members of a unit with respect to a common attribute X."[1] Common attributes include gender, ethnicity, professional status, and educational degree. A team is considered diverse if its members differ in respect to at least one attribute. Conceptually, Klein and Harrison grouped diversity into three basic groups—separation, disparity, and variety—which provides a helpful starting point. Here are three common boundaries that often confront teaming in complex organizations:

- **Physical distance:** *Separation diversity* includes differences in location—different time zones or the building down the street.

- **Status:** *Disparity diversity* ranks people according to the social value of a particular attribute. Teaming often confronts differences in status between people who need to work together to get a job done.

- **Knowledge:** *Variety diversity* describes differences in experience, knowledge, expertise, or education. When teaming, the major boundaries confronted in this category are differences in knowledge based on organizational membership or expertise.

The following sections look at examples of each of these types of boundaries and consider their impact on collaboration. Of course, sometimes people must cross multiple boundaries at once, such as when two team members have differences in terms of nationality, profession, gender, and time zone. Fortunately, leadership that helps establish process discipline and good communication can help overcome the challenges.

Physical Distance

An increasingly common teaming challenge is created by the need to span geographic distance. In many global companies, work teams in geographically dispersed locations all over the world, so-called virtual teams, are relied on to integrate expertise. A virtual team is a group of individuals who work across physical and organizational boundaries through the use of technology. Geographic regions in some organizations present nearly impermeable boundaries, even within the same country. At the Internal Revenue Service (IRS), for example, before Commissioner Charles Rossotti led the agency in an ambitious organizational transformation during his five-year tenure under President Bill Clinton, regional centers had acted like fiefdoms for decades, sharing neither information nor resources, despite the need to do both. Service representatives were unable to respond to the volume and variety of complex tax questions that would come into the regional center. The result was poor service and frustrated customers. Rossotti took down the regional barriers by combining all service representatives into one centralized national call center. Employees did not physically move. They still lived and worked in the old geographic locations, but they became part of one large virtual service team that was able to spread the workload in sensible and equitable ways. This organizational change enabled taxpayers' technical queries to be routed to those individuals with expertise in a particular aspect of the tax code—no matter where they were located.

Status

Disparity diversity may be the most challenging boundary to cross in teaming. When those at the top have the most power and those at the bottom have the least, lower-power individuals usually find it hard to speak up. Perhaps the most common power differences within work teams are professional status and ethnicity. Professional status can significantly affect beliefs about taking interpersonal risks and speaking up. In health care, for example, physicians have more status and power than nurses, who in turn have more status than technicians. Yet members of these professions often must team to take care of patients. Even people from the same profession can have status differences. Consider resident-level and senior ("attending") physicians working together to care for patients. Fears about taking interpersonal risk can prohibit candid discussion and hinder collaboration.

Note that demographic differences (differences based on gender, race, religion, and other social categories), which may readily be seen as variety diversity, sometimes also enforce a power hierarchy due to the nature of social power in various cultures and countries. For example, power and status differences in organizations have been documented for both gender and race. In addition, individuals aware of negative stereotypes associated with cultural identity may become hindered by self-fulfilling prophecies or a perceived need to overcome negative stereotypes. Similarly, unconscious negative stereotypes significantly hinder group performance because individuals tend to skirt or avoid the issue, allowing negative stereotypes to arise in other, more subtle ways.

Knowledge

Work teams often confront differences in expertise. In product and process development teams, for example, it is increasingly common to bring together people from different organizational functions for a limited period of intense teaming. The value of teaming is that different experts bring different knowledge and skills to the collaborative task. In product development, engineering offers insight into design and technology; manufacturing into feasible production processes, accurate cost estimates, pilot and full-scale production; and marketing into customer receptivity, customer segments, product positioning, and product plans. Teaming is the process of integrating these diverse skill sets and perspectives, as well as coordinating timelines and transferring resources across groups, when appropriate. However, diverse groups often have difficulty accessing and managing disparate knowledge, for two reasons. Misunderstandings arise due to different meanings embedded in different disciplines, and mistrust arises between groups.

Teaming Across Common Boundaries

Sharing knowledge across boundaries may not be natural in large organizations, but it's certainly worth the effort. Successfully overcoming the obstacles of teaming across boundaries offers valuable learning for individuals and provides a vital competitive advantage for organizations. Working across the three types of boundaries described in the previous section requires attention to their unique challenges and to techniques for overcoming them. For reference, Table 4.1 summarizes these common boundaries and their accompanying tactics.

As shown in Table 4.1, physical and status differences arise from distance and hierarchy, respectively, whereas knowledge boundaries arise from two distinct origins: membership in different organizations and membership in different occupations. The following sections explore the implications of teaming across each boundary and present strategies for successful teaming and learning within diverse groups.

Table 4.1 Common Boundaries That Impede Teaming and Organizational Learning

Boundary Type	Physical Distance	Status	Knowledge-Based	
Arises due to …	Dispersed geographic locations	Hierarchy	Different organizations collaborating	Different experts collaborating
Composition of team:	Geographically dispersed team members	Different levels of power or status	From different companies or different sites within a company	Diverse skills and expertise from education or function
Team challenges:	Misunderstandings, miscommunication, and coordination difficulty	Social norms of deference to authority	Competing taken-for-granted assumptions derived from organizational goals or values / Competing incentives	Team member allegiance to expertise-based subgroups
Collaboration enabled by …	Periodic visits to other sites / Focus on shared goal / Knowledge repositories and exchanges	Leadership inclusiveness to minimize experienced status gaps	Explicitly sharing individual perspectives / Emphasizing value brought by each organization / Focus on shared goal	Proactive sharing of expertise-based knowledge / Use of boundary objects like drawings, models, and prototypes

Teaming Across Distance Boundaries

"Sharing is not a natural thing," said Benedikt Benenati, the organizational development director at the multinational food company Groupe Danone. With subsidiaries in 120 countries, Groupe Danone is a multinational corporation that sought to promote teaming across the geographical boundaries of its many divisions. In addition to sharing common problems, such as getting retailers to stock the right amounts of Danone products at the right time, managers in different countries were focused on their own regions, and they rarely considered the opportunity to seek ideas from their counterparts in other regions. As Benenati pointed out, the company's senior managers may be part of the problem: "Managers may be reluctant to let their teams discuss among themselves. If members of their team find solutions, then perhaps managers are of no further use." Such reactions and fears are very human, of course, but they also leave opportunities for small process improvements around the globe to go untapped.

The information technology that enables us to shrink global distances by sending emails hurtling through cyberspace and to fax documents to machines across continents gives us a false sense of security, lulling us into believing that teamwork among geographically dispersed employees requires nothing more than a fast internet connection or new videoconferencing equipment. In fact, there are substantial barriers to sharing and integrating knowledge that virtual teams must overcome. In some organizations, however, it's the different mindsets across geographic regions, rather than the actual physical distance between them, that present nearly impermeable boundaries. In addition to the obvious challenges brought on by language and time zone differences, some types of knowledge just do not travel well. This is because certain, often very valuable, information is taken for granted by those who are closest to it. This tacit knowledge can be situated in ways that make it invisible to distant team members.

Teaming Across Status Boundaries

Most organizations contain vestiges of hierarchical boundaries. Although a command-and-control model of authority may have been productive in the past, the knowledge economy increasingly requires interactive communication and collaboration. The principal strategy for developing the necessary level of collaboration is leadership inclusiveness, in which higher-status individuals in a group actively invite and express appreciation for the views of others.

Consider the case of Patti Bondurant, senior clinical director at the Regional Center for Newborn Intensive Care at Cincinnati Children's Hospital. Bondurant felt that having the respiratory therapists, rather than the physician-director of the unit, lead an improvement project was a key driver to their improvement. She described this new relationship as follows:

> The turning point for us was when our respiratory therapy clinical managers in all three of the units said, "With all due respect, doctor, this is our expertise and you need to let us do our job." It was a really defining moment for this group. The doctor sat back and said, "I believe you're right. I don't need to hang onto control when there are people willing to do the work." . . . Those doctors were open to say, "Yes, you're the experts and we're going to let you do your job." The dynamic shifted from doctor sitting at the head of the table, to all of us becoming common denominators at the table.[2]

This is a textbook moment of teaming across hierarchical boundaries. The respiratory therapy clinical managers, lowest on the ladder, felt valued enough to speak clearly and directly to their institutional superiors with both expertise and a point of view. The doctors, at the top of the ladder, were able to sit back, listen, agree, and learn, thereby relinquishing control over every aspect of the project. Most important, spanning this boundary enabled a renegotiation of responsibilities, which in turn enabled improved care for the newborn patients.

Teaming Across Knowledge Boundaries

Organization and occupation are two important sources of knowledge boundaries. The former exists anytime people from different companies—or even sites within companies as we saw at the IRS—have to work together. The latter is driven by differences in areas of expertise, within and between organizations.

Organization-Based

Organizational membership brings with it taken-for-granted, or tacit, knowledge shared by other members of the same organization. People working together acquire shared experiences and practices that begin to seem (to them) like the obvious right way to do things. This tacit knowledge might consist of expectations about a particular supplier's reliability, the performance of a particular piece of equipment, or even awareness of who knows what in a given facility. Some things you just have to be on site to know. And because this kind of knowledge is taken for granted, people often don't realize that what they know is important to share. It is also the case that these kinds of knowledge boundaries often coexist with distance boundaries, which further raises the communication hurdle.

Consider the example of a new product development team in a large highly technical business charged with carrying out a project to develop a polymer for a new customer in a strategic market sector. With seven people dispersed across five sites on three continents, teleconferencing enabled the team to share extensive brainstorming and discussion, yet one ingredient for the new polymer proved unexpectedly difficult to source. One member of the team, an engineer in the United Kingdom whom I'll call David Thompson, turned to his local, on-site colleagues for help. As Thompson tells it, he was "just talking" when a colleague at his site happened to mention that he was making the difficult-to-source ingredient and could reserve a barrel for Thompson's team. It's the "just talking" around the proverbial watercooler that is situational, often crucial, and easily misunderstood by distant colleagues.

Occupation-Based

Training for any one profession is often a long process of mastering a specialized body of knowledge, terminology, and, above all, a mindset or way of knowing. Business students learn about marketing, management, and how to interpret company problems. Medical students learn about ligaments, blood vessels, and how to recognize disease. Writers learn about how to use language. Each profession is trained to make particular assumptions and epistemological assertions, which often become taken for granted. Jargon, acquired in specialized education and practice, often means that occupations speak different languages. This makes sharing across the "thought worlds" of occupational communities highly vulnerable to misunderstanding. In many cases, meaning is lost, errors are made, and synergy fails to materialize.

Expertise diversity is a key source of innovation. Individuals from different groups weave their ideas and knowledge into new, integrated forms. This type of synthesis is tricky even in mature industries, but particularly when confronting new or novel problems. Colocation, along with a lot of communication, and excitement about the innovative building they were trying to build, were essential to the team's ability to build trust across occupational boundaries that had long been antagonistic in the industry. Working across occupational boundaries is replete with technical and interpersonal challenges. It also comes with the territory of cross-functional teams.

Teams with occupational and expertise differences aligned with organizational departments or functions are called *cross-functional teams*. Such teams are on the rise in organizations, especially for innovation projects. The goal of cross-functional teaming is to bring together experts of various kinds who can combine knowledge gleaned from their distinct training to produce results that can't be achieved by any single discipline. Cross-functional teams are useful in organizations because they serve as a mechanism for combining different sets of highly specialized skills into one cohesive group. The obvious benefit of this form of collaboration is the qualified, high-level information that can be provided by each team member.

Research has shown that the challenge of occupational boundary spanning can be mitigated through the use of what are called *boundary objects* around which diverse groups can coalesce. Boundary objects like drawings, prototypes, and components are tangible representations of knowledge. Professor Paul Carlile of Boston University studied knowledge barriers in new product development teams in the automotive industry. He found that boundary objects facilitated spanning occupation and expertise boundaries. By pointing to and discussing elements in a model or schematic, the obfuscating qualities of jargon can be overcome. Similarly, University of California, Davis, professor Beth Bechky has found that while working face-to-face in a production, facility engineers, technicians, and assemblers can cocreate meaning, reaching across the boundaries between practices to do so. This process, which generates fuller understanding of the products and problems they face, involves more than just discussion but also shared action, for example, convening around a common machine or drawing to articulate different perspectives and develop a shared understanding. It also facilitates sharing expertise-based knowledge.

Occupation and Organization Combined

When knowledge boundaries based on expertise or profession are confounded with knowledge boundaries that exist between companies, the challenge intensifies. A complex building project, for example, brings together multiple areas of expertise as well as multiple companies to produce a customized product with unique constraints and goals. Participants in this process—owners, architects, engineers, and builders—have traditionally managed the manifold risks they face through legal contracts rather than through teaming, leaving the industry with a history of deep mistrust between professions.

Some recent innovative building projects have attempted to change the counterproductive dynamics in the construction industry by teaming across boundaries from the beginning of a project until the very end. The goal is to avoid the small failures that are nearly inevitable in complex, unique projects, and, of course, to avoid large failures, too. My colleague Faaiza Rashid and I studied a project that employed such an approach, called Integrated Project Delivery. Individuals from the multiple companies and professions in a large building project agreed to work together closely from project start to completion. Locating together in one workplace near the building site, everyone signed a single legal contract. Despite aggressive targets in budget, deadline, aesthetics, and environmental sustainability that made the project especially challenging, the teaming worked, trust grew, and the result was an award-winning building for the Boston area headquarters of software company Autodesk.

Teaming across boundaries of all kinds has the potential to help participants increase their knowledge of other fields. Working in diverse teams can expand participants' networks of colleagues from other areas of the organization and improve their boundary-spanning skills. This last point is particularly important because most teams must work across more than one diversity type or organizational boundary to solve today's most complex problems.

Team Across Boundaries

Every team must cross many kinds of boundaries to work effectively. Use this activity to think about the boundaries you have faced or are likely to face in your work.

Activity

Reflect on the following questions:

What are the three types of boundaries? Which have you had experience working across?

_____

_____

_____

How has specialization increased the need for teaming across boundaries?

_____

_____

_____

What type of boundary do you find most challenging to work across? Why?

_____

_____

_____

Wrap-Up

Performance goal: Get ready to learn, innovate, and compete.

Teaming and its associated interpersonal behaviors support organizational learning and require the right leadership mindset to optimize outcomes. This way of working allows employees to grow personally and professionally, whereas traditional top-down and assembly line models treated workers like children who must be told what to do.

Questions

1. Although teaming is imperative in today's organizations, neither teams nor organizations naturally do it well. Have you had an experience with unsuccessful teaming in your career?

2. There are several benefits to teaming. These benefits fall into two categories: better organizational performance and more engaging and satisfying work environments. Which category do you think is more important?

Activity

For this activity, get a paper and pen to write answers to these prompts.

Teaming is a dynamic way of working that provides the necessary coordination and collaboration without the luxury (or rigidity) of stable team structures. Do you see benefits to this approach? What about drawbacks? Do the benefits outweigh the drawbacks in your opinion? Why or why not?

Boundary spanning involves deliberate attempts to reach across the barriers that exist within and between groups of all kinds. Rapid developments in technology and the greater emphasis on globalization have greatly increased the significance of boundary spanning in today's work environment. What actions would you take to help span boundaries, such as workers located in different areas around the country or world?

Days 31–60

Performance goal: Team fearlessly with psychological safety.

Teaming is the art of communicating and coordinating with people across boundaries of all kinds: expertise, status, and distance, to name the most important. But whether you're teaming with new colleagues all the time or working in a stable team, effective teamwork happens best in a psychologically safe workplace.

The following table summarizes the goals you will pursue over the next 30 days. To keep yourself motivated, consider your personal goals and vision for success. What does psychological safety mean to you?

Days 31–60	
Performance Goal: Team fearlessly with psychological safety.	
Week 5	**Benchmark Goal: Grasp the power of psychological safety.** • Can you think of the last time you made an "unconscious calculation" to stay silent because of a lack of psychological safety? • What would have been different if you'd felt psychologically safe? • What does a psychologically safe workplace look like to you? • How does psychological safety boost performance?

Days 31–60
Performance Goal: Team fearlessly with psychological safety.

Week 6	**Benchmark Goal: Make it safe to team.** • What risks do you face at work? • What are some of the benefits of psychological safety? • Can you think of a time when hierarchy affected psychological safety for the worse? • Of the tools for cultivating psychological safety, which do you think you need to improve on the most?
Week 7	**Benchmark Goal: Frame your team for success.** • What is framing versus reframing? • What's a leader's role in framing? • How does framing play a role in teaming?
Week 8	**Benchmark Goal: Create a fearless organization.** • What's the leader's toolkit for creating a fearless organization? • How do you set the stage for psychological safety? • How do you get your organization excited about establishing psychological safety?

Personal Goals and Vision for Success
What do you hope to achieve by leveling up?
How could your life change by reaching these goals?

Teaming Without Fear

Benchmark goal: Grasp the power of psychological safety.

The tiny newborn twins seemed healthy enough, but their early arrival at only 27 weeks' gestation meant they were considered high-risk. Fortunately, the medical team at the busy urban hospital where the babies were delivered included staff from the neonatal intensive care unit (NICU): a young neonatal nurse practitioner named Christina Price (all names in this story are pseudonyms) and a silver-haired neonatologist named Dr. Drake. As Christina looked at the babies, she was concerned. Her recent training had included, as newly established best practice, administering a medicine (a prophylactic surfactant) that promoted lung development as soon as possible for a high-risk baby. Babies born very prematurely often arrive with lungs not quite ready for fully independent breathing outside the womb. But the neonatologist had not issued an order for the medicine. Christina stepped forward to remind Dr. Drake about the surfactant and then caught herself. Last week she'd overheard him publicly berate another nurse for questioning one of his orders. She told herself that the twins would probably be fine—after all, the doctor probably had a reason for avoiding the surfactant, still considered a judgment call—and she dismissed the idea of bringing it up. Besides, he'd already turned on his heel, off for his morning rounds, white coat billowing.

Unconscious Calculations

In hesitating and then choosing not to speak up, Christina was making a quick, not entirely conscious, risk calculation—the kind of micro-assessment most of us make numerous times a day. Most likely she was not even aware that she had weighed the risk of being belittled or berated against the risk that the babies might in fact need the medication to thrive. She told herself the doctor knew better than she did, and she was not confident he would welcome her input. Inadvertently, she had done something psychologists call *discounting the future*—underweighting the more important issue of the patients' health, which would take some time to play out, and overweighting the importance of the doctor's possible response, which would happen immediately. Our spontaneous tendency to discount the future explains the prevalence of many unhelpful or unhealthy behaviors—whether eating that extra piece of chocolate cake or procrastinating on a challenging assignment—and the failure to speak up at work is an important and often overlooked example of this problematic tendency.

Like most people, Christina was spontaneously managing her image at work. As noted sociologist Erving Goffman argued in his seminal 1957 book, *The Presentation of the Self in Everyday Life*, as humans, we are constantly attempting to influence others' perceptions of us by regulating and controlling information in social interactions. We do this both consciously and subconsciously.

Put another way, no one wakes up in the morning excited to go to work and look ignorant, incompetent, or disruptive. These are called *interpersonal risks*, and they are what nearly everyone seeks to avoid, not always consciously. In fact, most of us want to look smart, capable, or helpful in the eyes of others. No matter what our line of work, status, or gender, all of us learn how to manage interpersonal risk relatively early in life. At some point during elementary school, children start to recognize that what others think of them matters, and they learn how to lower the risk of rejection or scorn. By the time we're adults, we're usually really good at it! So good, we do it without conscious thought. Don't want to look ignorant? Don't ask questions. Don't want to look incompetent? Don't admit to mistakes or weaknesses. Don't want to be called "disruptive"? Don't make suggestions. While it might be acceptable at a social event to privilege looking good over making a difference, at work this tendency can lead to significant problems—ranging from thwarted innovation to poor service to, at the extreme, loss of human life. Yet avoiding behaviors that might lead others to think less of us is pretty much second nature in most workplaces.

As influential management thinker Nilofer Merchant said about her early days as an administrator at Apple, "I used to go to meetings and see the problem so clearly, when others could not." But worrying about being "wrong," she "kept quiet and learned to sit on my hands lest they rise up and betray me. I would rather keep my job by staying within the lines than say something and risk looking stupid." In one study investigating employee experiences with speaking up, 85 percent of respondents reported at least one occasion when they felt unable to raise a concern with their bosses, even though they believed the issue was important.

If you think this behavior is limited to those lower in the organization, consider the chief financial officer recruited to join the senior team of a large electronics company. Despite grave reservations about a planned acquisition of another company, the new executive said nothing. His colleagues seemed uniformly enthusiastic, and he went along with the decision. Later, when the takeover had clearly failed, the executives gathered with a consultant for a post-mortem. Each was asked to reflect on what they might have done to contribute to or avert the failure. The CFO, now less of an outsider, shared his earlier concerns, acknowledging that he had let the team down by not speaking up. Openly apologetic and emotional, he lamented that the others' enthusiasm had left him afraid to be "the skunk at the picnic."

The problem with sitting on our hands and staying within the lines rather than speaking up is that although these behaviors keep us personally safe, they can make us underperform and become dissatisfied. They can also put the organization at risk. In the case of Christina and the newborns, fortunately, no immediate damage was done, but the fear of speaking up can lead to accidents that were in fact avoidable. Remaining silent due to fear of interpersonal risk can make the difference between life and death. Airplanes have crashed, financial institutions have fallen, and hospital patients have died unnecessarily because individuals were, for reasons having to do with the climate in which they worked, afraid to speak up. Fortunately, it doesn't have to happen.

Envisioning the Psychologically Safe Workplace

Had Christina worked in a hospital unit where she felt psychologically safe, she would not have hesitated to ask the neonatologist whether or not he thought treating the newborns with prophylactic lung medicine was warranted. Here, too, she might not even be aware of making a conscious decision to speak up; it would simply seem natural to check. She would take for granted that her voice was appreciated, even if what she said didn't lead to a change in the patient's care. In a climate characterized by psychological safety—which blends trust and respect—the neonatologist might quickly agree with Christina and call the pharmacy to put in a request, or he might have explained why he thought it wasn't warranted in this case. Either way, the unit would be better off as a result. The patients would have received life-saving medication, or the team would have learned more about the subtleties of neonatal medicine. Before leaving the room, the doctor might thank Christina for her intervention. He'd be glad he could rely on her to speak up in case he slipped up, missed a detail, or was simply distracted.

Finally, as she gave the medicine to the babies, Christina might come up with the idea that the NICU could institute a protocol to make sure that that all babies who need a surfactant would get it. She might seek out her manager to make this suggestion during a break in the action. And because psychological safety exists in work groups, rather than between specific individuals (such as Christina and Dr. Drake), it's likely her nurse manager would be receptive to her suggestion.

Speaking up describes back-and-forth exchanges people have at work—from volunteering a concern in a meeting to giving feedback to a colleague. It also includes electronic communication (for example, sending an extra email to ask a coworker to clarify a particular point or seek help with a project). Valuable forms of speaking up include raising a different point of view in a conference call, asking a colleague for feedback on a report, admitting that a project is over budget or behind schedule, and so on—the myriad verbal interactions that make up the world of twenty-first century work.

There is, of course, a range of interpersonal riskiness involved in speaking up. Some cases of speaking up occur after significant trepidation; others feel reasonably straightforward and feasible. Still others simply don't occur—as in the case of Christina in the NICU—because one has weighed the risk (consciously or not) and come out on the side of silence. The free exchange of ideas, concerns, or questions is routinely hindered by interpersonal fear far more often than most managers realize. This kind of fear cannot be directly seen. Silence—when voice was possible—rarely announces itself! The moment passes, and no one is the wiser except the person who held back.

I have defined psychological safety as the belief that the work environment is safe for interpersonal risk-taking. The concept refers to the experience of feeling able to speak up with relevant ideas, questions, or concerns. Psychological safety is present when colleagues trust and respect each other and feel able—even obligated—to be candid.

In workplaces with psychological safety, the kinds of small and potentially consequential moments of silence experienced by Christina are far less likely. Speaking up occurs instead, facilitating the open and authentic communication that shines the light on problems, mistakes, and opportunities for improvement and increases the sharing of knowledge and ideas.

As you will see, our understanding of interpersonal risk management at work has advanced since Goffman studied the fascinating micro-dynamics of face saving. We now know that psychological safety emerges as a property of a group, and that groups in organizations tend to have very interpersonal climates. Even in a company with a strong corporate culture, you will find pockets of both high and low psychological safety. Take, for instance, the hospital where Christina works. One patient care unit might be a place where nurses readily speak up to challenge or inquire about care decisions, while in another it feels downright impossible. These differences in workplace climate shape behavior in subtle but powerful ways.

An Accidental Discovery

As much as I'm passionate about these ideas, I didn't set out to study psychological safety on purpose. As a first-year doctoral student in the process of clarifying my research interests for my eventual dissertation, I had been fortunate to join a large team studying medical error in several hospitals. This was a great way to gain research experience and to sharpen my general interest in how organizations can learn and succeed in an increasingly challenging, fast-paced world. I had long been interested in the idea of learning from mistakes for achieving excellence.

My role in the research team was to examine the effects of teamwork on medical error rates. The team had numerous experts, including physicians who could judge whether human error had occurred and trained nurse investigators who would review medical charts and interview frontline caregivers in patient care units in two hospitals to obtain error rates for each of these teams. These experts were, in effect, getting the data for what would be the dependent variable in my study—the team-level error rates. This was a great arrangement for me, for at least two reasons. First, I lacked the medical expertise to identify medical errors on my own. Second, from a research methods perspective, it meant that my survey measures of team effectiveness would not be subject to experimenter bias—the cognitive tendency for a researcher to see what they want to see rather than what is actually there. So the independence of our data collection activities was an important strength of the study.

The nurse investigators collected error data over a six-month period. During the first month, I distributed a validated instrument called the *team diagnostic survey* to everyone working in the study units—doctors, nurses, and clerks—slightly altering the language of the survey items to make sure they would make sense to people working in a hospital, and adding a few new items to assess people's views about making mistakes. I also spent time on the floor (in the patient care units) observing how each of the teams worked.

Going into the study, I hypothesized, not surprisingly, that the most effective teams would make the fewest errors. Of course, I had to wait six months for the data on the dependent variable (the error rates) to be fully collected. And here is where the story took an unexpected turn.

First, the good news (from a research perspective anyway). There was variance! Error rates across teams were strikingly different; indeed, there was a 10-fold difference in the number of human errors per 1,000 patient days (a standard measure) from the best to the worst unit on what I sincerely believed was an important performance measure. A wrong medicine dose, for example, might be reported every three weeks on one ward but every other day on another. Likewise, the team survey data also showed significant variance. Some teams were much stronger—their members reported more mutual respect, more collaboration, more confidence in their ability to deliver great results, more satisfaction, and so on—than others.

When all of the error and survey data were compiled, I was at first thrilled. Running the statistical analysis, I immediately saw that there was a significant correlation between the independently collected error rates and the measures of team effectiveness from my survey. But then I looked closely and noticed something wrong. The direction of the correlation was exactly the opposite of what I had predicted. Better teams were apparently making more—not fewer—mistakes than less strong teams. Worse, the correlation was statistically significant. I briefly wondered how I could tell my dissertation chair the bad news. This was a problem.

No, it was a puzzle.

Did better teams really make more mistakes? I thought about the need for communication between doctors and nurses to produce safe, error-free care. The need to ask for help, to double-check each other's work to make sure, in this complex and customized work environment, that patients received the best care. I knew that great care meant that clinicians had to team up effectively. It just didn't make sense that good teamwork would lead to more errors. I wondered for a moment whether better teams got overconfident over time and then became sloppy. That might explain my perplexing result. But why else might better teams have higher error rates?

84

And then came the eureka moment. What if the better teams had a climate of openness that made it easier to report and discuss error? The good teams, I suddenly thought, don't *make* more mistakes; they *report* more. But having this insight was a far cry from proving it.

I decided to hire a research assistant to go out and study these patient care teams carefully, with no preconceptions. He didn't know which units had made more mistakes, or which ones scored better on the team survey. He didn't even know my new hypothesis. In research terms, he was "blind" to both the hypothesis and the previously collected data.

Here is what he found. Through quiet observation and open-ended interviews about all aspects of the work environment, he discovered that the teams varied wildly in whether people felt able to talk about mistakes. And these differences were almost perfectly correlated with the detected error rates. In short, people in the better teams (as measured by my survey, but unbeknownst to the research assistant) talked openly about the risks of errors, often trying to find new ways to catch and prevent them. It would take another couple of years before I labeled this climate difference *psychological safety*. But the accidental finding set me off on a new and fruitful research direction: to find out how interpersonal climate might vary across groups in other workplaces, and whether it might matter for learning and speaking up in other industries—not just in health care.

Over the years, in studies in companies, hospitals, and even government agencies, my doctoral students and I have found that psychological safety does indeed vary, and that it matters very much for predicting both learning behavior and objective measures of performance. Today, researchers like me have conducted dozens of studies showing greater learning, performance, and even lower mortality as a result of psychological safety.

In that initial study over two decades ago, I learned that psychological safety varies across groups within hospitals. Since that time, I have replicated this finding in many industry settings. The data are consistent in this simple but interesting finding: psychological safety seems to live at the level of the group. In other words, in the organization where you work, it's likely that different groups have different interpersonal experiences; in some, it may be easy to speak up and bring your full self to work. In others, speaking up might be experienced as a last resort—as it did in some of the patient care teams I studied. That's because psychological safety is very much shaped by local leaders.

Understanding Psychological Safety

Psychological safety makes it possible to give tough feedback and have difficult conversations without the need to tiptoe around the truth. In psychologically safe environments, people believe that if they make a mistake, others will not penalize or think less of them for it. This activity explores your own experience with psychological safety in the workplace.

Activity

Reflect on the following questions:

Can you think of a time at work when you made a conscious or unconscious calculation to stay silent rather than speaking up? What held you back from speaking up?

_____

_____

_____

How do you spontaneously manage your image at work? What kind of image do you try to project? How does that lead to actions (or nonactions) that may negatively affect the quality of the work in your team or organization?

_____

_____

_____

Have you worked on a psychologically safe team? Do you agree that such an environment makes it easier to report errors?

_____

_____

_____

Creating Psychological Safety

Benchmark goal: Make it safe to team.

On January 16, 2003, the space shuttle *Columbia* was successfully launched from the Kennedy Space Center on a 16-day research mission. The next day, shuttle engineer Rodney Rocha reviewed a video of the launch and became deeply concerned about the size and position of a chunk of insulating foam that appeared to have fallen off the shuttle's external tank and struck its left wing. The video images were grainy, and it was impossible to be sure what had happened. To determine whether damage had occurred, Rocha hoped to obtain photographic images of the shuttle's wing from spy satellites. Although the photos would have to be authorized by the Air Force, the request would require neither a technical nor financial miracle. It did mean that NASA would have to ask for help from the Department of Defense.

Rocha initially expressed the need for the satellite images in an email to his immediate superior, emphasizing the urgency by using boldfaced type. When he learned that his request was unlikely to be honored, Rocha wrote a scathing email: "Remember the NASA safety poster everywhere around, stating, 'If it's not safe, say so?' Yes, it's that serious." He didn't send the email to the mission manager, however;

he only shared it with fellow engineers. Later, he explained that "engineers were often told not to send messages much higher than their own rung in the ladder."

Discouraged by his early efforts to call attention to the foam-strike issue and convinced that voicing concerns was career limiting at NASA, Rocha refrained from sharing his anxiety in a critical mission management team meeting, eight days into the flight. He fervently hoped others with more clout might offer their concerns. The opportunity passed, however, and the issue was never formally revisited in a mission management team meeting.

Just eight days after this lost opportunity to speak up, the shuttle burned up on reentry into the Earth's atmosphere, resulting in the death of all seven astronauts. Much later, asked in a television interview with ABC News anchor Charlie Gibson why he didn't voice his doubts about the safety of the shuttle in that mission management team meeting, Rocha replied, "I just couldn't do it. I'm too low down . . . and she [mission management team leader Linda Ham] is way up here," gesturing with his hand held above his head.

The 2003 *Columbia* space shuttle tragedy reflects an unusually dramatic consequence of not speaking up in the workplace—especially with tentative concerns or unproven ideas—an all-too-common organizational dynamic. Instances where people are reluctant to voice concerns or engage in behaviors that could threaten their image occur within a wide spectrum of industries and organizations. Although it's understandable to keep silent about mistakes when not much is at stake, in many situations errors can be deadly.

The term *psychological safety* describes a climate in which people feel free to express relevant thoughts and feelings. Although it sounds simple, the ability to seek help and tolerate mistakes while colleagues watch can be unexpectedly difficult. Yet, frank conversations and public missteps must occur if teaming is to realize the promise of collaboration across differences.

Promoting Trust and Respect

Simply put, psychological safety makes it possible to give tough feedback and have difficult conversations without the need to tip-toe around the truth. In psychologically safe environments, people believe that if they make a mistake others will not penalize or think less of them for it. They also believe that others will not resent or humiliate them when they ask for help or information. This belief comes about when people both trust and respect each other, and it produces a sense of confidence that the group won't embarrass, reject, or punish someone for speaking up. Thus psychological safety is a taken-for-granted belief about how others will respond when you ask a question, seek feedback, admit a mistake, or propose a possibly wacky idea. Most people feel a need to manage interpersonal risk to retain a good image, especially at work, and especially in the presence of those who formally evaluate them. This need is both instrumental (promotions and rewards may depend on impressions held by bosses and others) and socio-emotional (we simply prefer approval over disapproval).

Psychological safety does not imply a cozy situation in which people are necessarily close friends. Nor does it suggest an absence of pressure or problems. Psychological safety does not mean a group has to be cohesive or in agreement about things. As research has shown, group cohesiveness can reduce people's willingness to disagree with or challenge each other. The term *groupthink* refers to this problem. Specifically, in many cohesive groups, people are reluctant to disturb the feeling of harmony created by the group's apparent agreement about an important issue. This leads them to hold back or fail to admit to holding a different view, and thus contributes to poor decision-making. Yale professor Irving Janis attributed President Kennedy's ill-fated plan to send Cuban exiles to invade the Bay of Pigs in 1961 to groupthink. By contrast, psychological safety describes a

Creating Psychological Safety

climate in which raising a dissenting view is expected and welcomed. A tolerance of dissent enables productive discussion and early detection of problems.

I have found that many people are genuinely pained and frustrated by keeping silent at work. For the most part, the people I've studied aren't failing to provide ideas or input because they've "checked out" or don't care, but because of a subtle but pervasive fear of what others, particularly those in power, might think of them. As most people intuitively recognize, each of us engages in a tacit calculus in which we assess the risk associated with a given interpersonal behavior, quickly and effortlessly, as we face a micro-behavior decision point. To illustrate what I mean by a micro-behavior decision point, imagine that while you are in a conversation with your boss, you consider fleetingly, "Should I say something about this?" In this almost imperceptible thinking process, you weigh the potential gain against the potential loss. You wonder, "If I do this, will I be hurt, embarrassed, or criticized?" If you quickly conclude that the answer is no, then you have a sense of psychological safety, and you proceed to voice your thoughts. (If you believe that the answer might be that you could be hurt but you speak anyway, then you are demonstrating courage.) Typically, proceeding means being authentic. It means expressing the work-relevant thoughts and feelings on your mind without excessive self-censorship.

Consider the fact that admitting a mistake or asking for help may be unthinkable in one work setting and yet readily accepted, even valued, in another setting. The difference between the two situations is what psychological safety is all about.

The easy solution to minimizing image risk at work is to avoid doing or saying anything unless you're absolutely sure you're right. This is obviously a facetious solution. Not only does it limit creativity, stifle innovation, and preclude authentic relationships but it also creates important risks of another kind: risks to performance and safety. This is especially true in dangerous industries such as nuclear power, where admitting errors and asking for help may be critical for avoiding catastrophe. The human tendency to favor silence over voicing concerns is also particularly troubling in organizations where lives are at stake, such as in hospitals. Extensive research on hospitals and other high-risk organizations has shown that rules and required procedures are not enough to eradicate errors that were not caught or corrected due to a lack of psychological safety. This isn't because people deliberately break rules, but rather because of the subtle ways in which we make sense of uncertainty and view each other at work.

Weighing Interpersonal Risks in the Work Environment

Whether frequently or infrequently, overtly or implicitly, most people in organizations are being evaluated in an ongoing way. The presence of others with more power or status makes the threat associated with being evaluated especially powerful, but it by no means disappears in the presence of peers and subordinates.

The four following concerns powerfully shape our willingness to speak up:

- **Being seen as ignorant:** When individuals ask questions or seek information, they run the risk of being seen as ignorant. Most of us can think of a time when we hesitated to ask a question because it seemed that no one else was asking, or perhaps we believed the information was something we were already expected to know.

- **Being seen as incompetent:** When admitting mistakes, asking for help, or accepting the high probability of failure that comes with experimenting, people risk being seen as incompetent. For example, if you admit that something you tried didn't work as expected, it could possibly signal to others that you're not skilled or smart enough to reliably perform your job.

- **Being seen as negative:** To learn and improve, it's essential to critically evaluate current and past activities and performance. The risk of being seen as negative, however, often stops people from providing critical assessments. People often believe that critiquing others' performance will make them appear overly critical or hard to work with. In addition, it is well known that bad news rarely travels well up the hierarchy.

- **Being seen as disruptive:** Fearful of disrupting or imposing on others' time, people avoid seeking feedback, information, or help. In particular, individuals are often reluctant to seek feedback about their performance, despite the personal gains that can be obtained from feedback. Although this reluctance can be attributed to the possibility of hearing something negative, it also stems from a wish not to be seen as intrusive or lacking in self-sufficiency.

The Benefits of Psychological Safety

The benefits of psychological safety include the following:

- **Encourages speaking up:** Psychological safety alleviates concern about others' reaction to behaviors or actions that have the potential for embarrassment.

- **Enables clarity of thought:** When the brain is activated by fear, it has less neural processing power for exploration, design, or analysis.

- **Supports productive conflict:** Psychological safety enables self-expression, productive discussion, and the thoughtful handling of conflict.

- **Mitigates failure:** A climate of psychological safety makes it easier, and therefore more common, to report and discuss errors.

- **Promotes innovation:** Removing the fear of speaking up enables people to suggest the novel ideas and possibilities that are integral to developing innovative products and services.

- **Removes obstacles to pursuing goals for achieving performance:** With psychological safety, individuals can focus on achieving motivating goals rather than on self-protection.

- **Increases accountability:** Rather than supporting a permissive atmosphere, psychological safety creates a climate that supports people in taking the interpersonal risks necessary to pursue high standards and achieve challenging goals.

Those are clearly some powerful benefits. But how do you establish an environment of psychological safety?

Cultivating Psychological Safety

How do leaders raise the level of psychological safety in an organization? This is the question that Arthur Ryan, CEO of Prudential, asked himself after taking the 100-year-old insurance and investment company public. Ryan looked around at the increasingly complex and competitive financial services industry and concluded that the Prudential culture—dubbed *Pru-polite* by employees for its cautious feel—would have to change to succeed. In particular, Ryan believed that operating successfully as a public company would require direct, honest communication among employees. This meant creating a psychologically safe environment that enabled them to openly debate issues and analyze customer needs.

In an effort to increase levels of psychological safety, Ryan asked a team from the human resources department to create a program focused on encouraging employees to speak up and share their thoughts. Calling the program the *Safe-to-Say* initiative, the team worked energetically to design and implement a series of integrated training programs and recurring staff meetings that would make the work climate more psychologically safe. Many at Prudential, including senior managers and frontline representatives, spoke positively of the efforts, but substantial change in the culture was slow. An internal survey revealed remarkably stable scores on items relevant to the ability to speak up. The primary lesson here: you cannot metaphorically snap your fingers with short-term initiatives, no matter how well intentioned, and expect psychologically safety to suddenly exist.

Leadership Cultivating Psychological Safety

Leaders—at all levels, but particularly those in the middle of an organization—play crucial roles in creating a psychologically safe organization. The impact of leaders on organizational culture is well established by research. Studies have shown that leaders' responses to events influence other members' perceptions of appropriate and safe behavior. It's clear that signals sent by people in power are critical to shaping others' ability and willingness to offer their ideas and observations. When a leader of a team is supportive, coaching oriented, and nondefensive in response to questions and challenges, team members are likely to feel that the team constitutes a safe environment. By contrast, team leaders who act authoritarian or punitive reduce others' psychological safety and, as a consequence, hinder their ability to contribute everything they can to the collective effort.

The most important influence on psychological safety is the nearest manager, supervisor, or boss. These authority figures, in subtle and not so subtle ways, shape the tone of interactions in a team or group. Therefore, they also must be engaged as the primary drivers in establishing a more open work environment. They must take practical steps to make the workplace psychologically safe. That is the key phrase: take practical steps.

Be Accessible and Approachable

Leaders encourage team members to learn together by being accessible and personally involved. In one of the cardiac surgery teams I studied, an operating room nurse made this association by describing the surgeon leading her team as "very accessible. He's in his office, always just two seconds away. He can always take five minutes to explain something, and he never makes you feel stupid." In striking contrast, the surgeon in one of the less successful teams requested that nonphysician team members go through his residents (junior physicians who are still in training) if they had something to say, rather than speak to him directly. Through their behaviors, these two surgeons conveyed very different messages to their teams: the first surgeon increased the likelihood that people would speak up openly both in and outside of the operating room when they had concerns and questions, whereas the second surgeon obviously made the process of communication more difficult.

Acknowledge the Limits of Current Knowledge

Explicitly acknowledge the lack of answers to the tough problems your group or team faces. Strange as it may seem, many leaders are unwilling to publicly express the fact that they don't have the answers to every issue or challenge. It's not that they don't recognize the imperfect state of knowledge; they just fail to mention it. Acknowledging uncertainty may seem like a weakness, but in fact it's usually an intelligent and accurate diagnosis of a murky situation. Moreover, it creates an implied invitation to offer information or expertise.

Display Fallibility

To create psychological safety, team leaders must demonstrate a tolerance of failure by acknowledging their own fallibility. Self-disclosure by team leaders is an effective way to reveal one's limitations. For instance, one cardiac surgeon team leader in the previously mentioned study repeatedly told his team, "I need to hear from you because I'm likely to miss things." The repetition of the phrase was as important as its meaning. People tend not to hear or believe a message that contradicts old norms or stances when they hear it only once. Acknowledging one's fallibility and the need for feedback suggests to others that their opinion is respected and contributes to establishing a norm of active participation. Moreover, when managers and supervisors admit that they don't know something or made a mistake, their genuine display of humility encourages others to do the same.

Invite Participation

A logical extension of acknowledging limits and modeling fallibility is inviting others to offer observations and ideas. This means explicitly requesting input from other people on a team or in the organization more broadly. Team and organizational-level learning both depend on gaining access to a valuable, untapped body of individually held knowledge. Leaders must seek out this individual, internal knowledge, especially from lower-status team members who might otherwise be reluctant to speak. Team leaders can play a role in drawing out members' thoughts by setting up reflective sessions where job and time pressures are temporarily removed. In these types of sessions, ask questions. But be sure to ask real questions, not leading or rhetorical ones. When people believe leaders and managers want to hear from them and value their input, they're more responsive.

Highlight Failures as Learning Opportunities

By avoiding punishing others for having taken well-intentioned risks that backfired, leaders inspire people to embrace error and failure and deal with them in a productive manner. Vivid examples of purposefully refraining from penalizing failure exist throughout management literature. Apocryphal stories prevalent in many organizations capture the ways in which senior management can powerfully influence views of psychological safety in the organization as a whole. One such story involves Tom Watson Jr. at IBM and a field executive responsible for a $10 million mistake. Called into the chairman's office, the executive was understandably anxious. As retold by Paul Carroll, "Watson asked, 'Do you know why I've asked you here?' The man replied, 'I assume I'm here so you can fire me.' Watson looked surprised. 'Fire you?' he asked. 'Of course not. I just spent $10 million educating you.' He then reassured the executive and suggested he keep taking chances."

Truth or myth, such stories have lasting effects in an organization. The sent message is that failure is inevitable and the point is to learn, to share the learning, and to try again. As espoused by Watson, "You really aren't committed to innovation unless you're willing to fail. . . . The fastest way to succeed is to double your failure rate." One of the best-known examples is the story of 3M's wildly successful Post-it product. As nearly everyone has heard by now, the adhesive used in Post-it notes came from a botched attempt to create a super-strong adhesive. Similarly, a well-known public relations firm has a ritual of opening monthly meetings by recognizing the "Mistake of the Month." This is a lighthearted way to both build a sense of community and acknowledge the value of learning from mistakes.

Use Direct Language

In knowledge work, people can't afford to avoid critiques due to a fear of sounding negative, criticizing the boss, or making the company appear fallible. Strategy teams, new product development, and other project teams often face crucial decisions that require evaluating the current situation and suggesting difficult changes. A major challenge in these discussions is to be objective and blunt. Often, however, the language is anything but direct. For example, the top management team of a manufacturing company that I studied engaged in a series of meetings to develop a new strategy. In these conversations, I observed a persistent pattern of using metaphors, rather than direct language, to describe the company's strategic options. As one executive commented during one meeting:

> Listening to Bob talk about the ship, I'd like to explore the difference between the metaphor of the ship and how the rudder gets turned and when, in contrast to a flotilla, where there's lots of little rudders and we're trying to orchestrate the flotilla. I think this contrast is important. At one level, we talk about this ship and all the complexities of trying to determine not only its direction but also how

to operationalize the ship in total to get to a certain place, versus allowing a certain degree of freedom that the flotilla analogy evokes.

Although metaphors can provoke new ideas and elicit creativity, they can sometimes obscure the real issues and preclude direct or contentious discussion. In this team, members rarely asked for clarification of each other's words or tried to identify areas of disagreement. Instead, the team continued to discuss the company and its situation abstractly, avoiding disagreement and postponing resolution. By the end of six months of regular meetings, little progress had been made; the team's abstract ruminations had failed to translate into any sort of action.

Set Boundaries

Paradoxically, when leaders are as clear as possible about what constitutes blameworthy acts, people feel more psychologically safe than when boundaries of acceptable action are subject to guesswork. This means leaders must establish and clarify boundaries at the outset of a teaming or learning effort. In a financial institution, this may mean never exceeding a particular investment limit without approval. In a hospital setting, it may mean never failing to ask for help when there is any doubt about a patient's condition or medication. For the team at Motorola, it meant never violating the code of secrecy about the project, until the product was publicly unveiled. Establishing this clear restriction helped promote a sense of freedom and expression within the delineated boundaries, including the willingness to ignore the recommendations of human factors experts about the phone's width. Regardless of the situation, by setting clear boundaries for action and behavior within the team, leaders contribute to building an environment of psychological safety.

Hold People Accountable

It's the job of leaders to help people understand that unacceptable behaviors do occur and must be equitably addressed. When leaders take the difficult step of punishing or even firing someone, they must clearly explain what happened and why, while observing rules for confidentiality as appropriate. Providing the justification behind such difficult actions helps protect other people against fear that the actions were arbitrary and could happen to them, without warning. In most cases, people understand both the rationale and the need for sanctions to preserve the team or organization's integrity so that it can effectively fulfill its purpose. Although it is more about avoiding the destruction of psychological safety than about creating it in the first place, holding people accountable builds fairness and responsibility, which removes the fear of leader arbitrariness. This is why psychological safety and accountability are both essential to a "just culture," an increasingly central concept in health care and other high-risk operations. The idea of a just culture was developed to acknowledge that "competent professionals make mistakes and . . . even develop unhealthy norms (shortcuts, 'routine rule violations')" while maintaining "zero tolerance for reckless behavior." In short, psychological safety is not created through lax standards or permissiveness, but rather through sober recognition that any workplace presents both challenges and constraints that must be discussed openly if progress is to be made.

Setting boundaries and holding people accountable are critical for a leader hoping to cultivate an environment of psychological safety. It may seem counterintuitive, but think of these two actions as being like guardrails on a bridge. If the guardrails are missing, you're likely to drive as close to the center line as possible. It's obviously frightening to drive near the bridge's edge without rails in place. When teaming and learning, the equivalent is sticking to safe, tractable behaviors that shield you from possible punishment, while avoiding behaviors with interpersonal risk, like admitting mistakes, that may be interpreted as "outside the lines." But when the guardrails are in place, there's less risk in venturing to the outside lanes and gaining a broader, more informed perspective. With clear boundaries and the structures that enforce them, you're more likely to test the limits of current processes and knowledge. In doing so, team members and teams greatly increase their ability to collaborate, learn, and innovate.

Setting the Stage for Psychological Safety

Psychological safety means no one will be punished or humiliated for errors or questions in the service of reaching ambitious performance goals. The following activity helps you probe your experiences and thoughts of psychological safety.

Activity
Reflect on the following questions:

Of the seven benefits of psychological safety, which do you think is most valuable in your current work?

_____

_____

_____

Has your organization or a past organization you worked for promoted psychological safety? Did the effort succeed or fail? Why?

_____

_____

_____

(continued)

Creating Psychological Safety

(continued)

If you are not in a leadership position, what can you do to promote psychological safety on your team? How might these actions matter? Why?

_____

_____

_____

Framing for Learning

Benchmark goal: Frame your team for success.

Teaming behavior is often at odds with the demands of formal organizational structures, which divide people by specialty and focus more of their attention on bosses than on peers. Natural cognitive biases can get in the way, too; for many kinds of knowledge work, effective teaming requires suspension of the spontaneous assumption that one's own perspective is more accurate than those of others. In many workplaces, therefore, engaging in teaming may feel like an unnatural act; thus, leadership is needed to create an environment conducive to teaming.

Framing is a crucial leadership action for enrolling people in any substantial behavior change. It is especially important for promoting teaming and learning. Framing helps people interpret the ambiguous signals that accompany change in a positive and productive light, and facilitates understanding of new performance expectations. This week, I explore what leaders can do to frame a new initiative or project in a way that supports successful teaming and engages people in the learning and problem-solving challenges that lie ahead.

Cognitive Frames

A *frame* is a set of assumptions or beliefs about a situation. Most of the time, framing occurs automatically. We rarely recognize the power of the automatic frames we've superimposed on situations, because we take them for granted. Frames nearly always exist, shaped by past experiences. Without our realizing it, these prior experiences affect how we think and feel about the current situation. Framing is neither bad nor good; it is simply inevitable. We interpret what is going on around us through an invisible lens shaped by our personal history and social context. The problem is that we tend to assume that our framing represents the truth, rather than merely presenting a subjective map. In truth, however, each frame offers its own image of reality.

Tacit Interpretations

In complex situations, such as a busy hospital ward, an improvement project, or a strategy session, people interpret ambiguous cues and draw conclusions about what is happening. Cognitive research shows that many of these effortlessly drawn interpretations are tacit (taken for granted, not explicitly recognized), yet extremely powerful. Once we interpret a situation, we think we know its true meaning. In addition, when we work closely with others, we develop shared interpretations, and these are also taken for granted. As a result, people in a particular workplace often look at what's going on through tacit, shared frames. In studies of workplace conversation, in particular, researchers have identified frames that shape how we talk to each other. These frames feel natural, but make it difficult for people to learn much from each other, especially when they have conflicting points of view. In a conflict, most people have a tacit goal of winning (few of us enter a conflict with a goal of learning as much as we can about the merits of the other person's point of view). Within this frame, conflict is viewed as a competition to be won rather than a problem to be understood and solved.

Others have used the term *mental model* or *taken-for-granted assumption* to convey a similar idea, but the terminology of framing applies particularly well to understanding teaming behavior. The terms *frame* and *framing* suggest the idea of looking through something at something else. A frame directs attention to features of the object of interest in a subtle way. Although our focus is on the painting, its frame can enhance or diminish our appreciation of the painting's colors and shapes without our conscious attention. Similarly, leaders and managers can use cognitive frames to highlight or encourage specific traits that help promote behaviors necessary for teaming and learning.

In a well-known example of the power of framing, Viktor Frankl, a Nazi concentration camp survivor, endured Auschwitz by imagining himself sharing the stories of courage he saw around him to friends and family on the outside. Frankl, a psychiatrist, later described the moment of transformation that enabled him to persevere in these worst of conditions: it was when he recognized the opportunity to reframe his experience from one of minute-to-minute suffering and fear to one of future-oriented visioning and hope. It's an extreme example, but Frankl's remarkable story of courage and resilience illustrates the potential consequences of reframing—seeing the same situation one way rather than another, very different way.

Reframing for Learning

Psychologists and behavioral scientists have established the power of a variety of alternative cognitive frames. For instance, when people frame a task as a "performance situation" they are more risk averse and less willing to persist through obstacles than when the same task is framed as a "learning situation." Not only do people adopting a learning frame persist longer in unfamiliar, challenging tasks but also they ultimately learn more as a result. In addition, people with a performance frame engage in less experimentation and innovation and are less likely to formulate new strategies in difficult situations. Instead, they're more likely to fall back on ineffective strategies they have used previously. Similarly, other research distinguishes between a "promotion" and a "prevention" orientation in approaching a task or challenge. A promotion orientation is characterized by ideals, goals, and eagerness to attain them. It reflects a tendency to frame new situations in terms of what can be gained. Conversely, a prevention orientation is characterized by a sense of obligation and by vigilance against loss. It indicates an inclination for framing new situations as opportunities to lose ground.

Fortunately, frames can be changed. Behavioral scientists and therapists have studied the process of reframing to help people change their tacit frames and obtain better results in their lives. One approach—rational behavioral therapy—teaches people to try out more productive, learning-oriented ways of framing themselves. Managerial research has also explored the process of framing, how it works, and how powerful it can be for improving results. Notably, Chris Argyris, one of the seminal scholars of organizational learning, conducted research over many years with managers to identify and challenge the tacit frames that shaped how they interacted with each other in difficult, confrontational conversations. Similarly, Donald Schön, another pioneering researcher and a longtime colleague of Argyris, showed that how people framed their roles shaped their behavior and, correspondingly, helped determine the results they achieved.

Team Members' Roles

When temporary teams form, it's natural for people to assume roles according to position, expertise, or personality. Due to this inevitability, thoughtfully framing the roles that different people should play in a joint effort is important to building a cohesive team and an effective process. In particular, in a setting where jobs have traditionally been highly segmented—such that task interdependence is managed in advance by clear role boundaries—making a shift to a way of working characterized by back-and-forth communication can be extremely challenging. Getting people to start teaming requires a new frame.

Intellectual and Emotional Commitment

A critical part of framing people's roles in a temporary team project is to communicate that they are being selected for the project for a reason. This builds intellectual and emotional commitment to the implementation process and acts as an invitation to others to participate in shaping the specifics of the effort, in addition to helping execute it. It also represents an implicit awareness that new technology imposes a need for change, that change is hard, and that everyone affects whether or not the change succeeds. When leaders emphasize that they have handpicked great people for a project, it builds intellectual and emotional commitment.

By contrast, when leaders fail to convey that others play vital roles in the project, team members may not believe they can or will make genuine contributions to its success. This compromises their ability to envision and help shape how a new technology or process can transform the work to help the organization or its customers. Framing powerfully influences commitment and motivates people to exert the effort and take the risks that change requires. These observations point to a simple but incontrovertible fact: teaming works when everyone makes it work. Learning happens when individuals commit to cooperating in a unified effort to overcome the inevitable setbacks that accompany innovation and implementation. Deliberate, positive reframing motivates team members to communicate more intensively, thus lessening the confines of hierarchy. Individual motives become more closely aligned with the purpose of the project.

The Project Purpose

Even when individual employees are aware of problems, a collective effort focused on solving them is unlikely to occur when people do not understand and care about a common purpose. Therefore, effectively framing a task involves providing a compelling answer to the question of why a particular project exists. What purpose does it serve? What value does the project offer to employees, customers, or society? The leader's job is to articulate and help people cohere around this shared purpose. Whether or not the effort to create a sense of purpose is effective hinges on the leader's ability to connect the teaming effort to goals and objectives that motivate people to persist during a novel, uncertain endeavor. Just as individuals have a promotion or prevention orientation, projects are often framed in either an aspirational or a defensive way.

Aspirational or Defensive Purpose

Many teams I've studied fell into one of two groups in terms of team beliefs—explicit or inferred—about the reason for implementing the new technology. Members of successful teams shared a sense of purpose that can be described as aspirational—driven by a desire to accomplish compelling goals. By contrast, unsuccessful teams' goals were fundamentally preventative and reactive. These teams were driven by concerns about competition and encumbered by the anxiety of coping with technological change. This latter belief seemed to be the default state in the absence of leadership effort to impose a new, inspiring belief.

Communicating a Clear and Compelling Purpose

Engaging others' willing contribution is a core leadership task. This means that leaders in uncertain, dynamic contexts have to stimulate and guide a collective learning process. To do so, leaders must communicate a clear and compelling purpose that resonates with all members of the team. The type of purpose that motivates teaming generally has meaning beyond making money or self-preservation, providing a clear, aspirational goal that energizes others and encourages a focus on collective responsibility for teaming and learning. An aspirational purpose encapsulates the excitement of doing something that aids others and helps team members endure the hardships of learning. By explicitly communicating growing confidence in a new process or technology, leaders ensure that team members recognize that they are making progress toward achieving the purpose.

Together, these three dimensions of framing—establishing the leader's role, others' roles, and a shared purpose—play a crucial part in determining success or failure in a substantial change effort. By helping shape others' perceptions of roles and objectives, deliberate framing can make the difference between the creation of an environment that supports collaboration and encourages persistence or a defensive environment that implicitly presents change as a burden to be endured. The framing makes all the difference between individuals who see themselves as embarking on a valued learning journey and those who are merely trying to get the work done.

A Learning Frame Versus an Execution Frame

Leaders who frame themselves as interdependent with others in accomplishing important changes, view others as crucial partners, and put forward an aspirational purpose are employing a learning frame. By contrast, leaders who present themselves as experts who are more important than others in completing the journey ahead, and see others as supporting actors, can be characterized as having an execution frame. Table 7.1 directly contrasts the three dimensions of a learning frame with those of an execution frame.

Table 7.1   Learning Frame Versus Execution Frame

Project Dimension	Learning Frame	Execution Frame
Leader's view of self in carrying out the project	Important and interdependent in overcoming the challenges ahead	Knows what to do and in a position to tell others what to do
Leader's view of others in carrying out the project	Valued partners with essential input for overcoming the challenges ahead	Coactors or subordinates
Overall view of the situation created by the project and corresponding tacit goal for the project	Challenging, full of unknowns, and an opportunity to try out new concepts and techniques; the tacit goal is to learn as much as possible so as to figure out what to do next	Same as, or "not that different from," normal situation; the tacit goal is to get the job done

When managing a project in which risk and uncertainty are high, leaders who employ and communicate a learning frame help launch a rewarding collaborative effort that promotes learning and innovation. By contrast, when, by design or by default, work is framed as an opportunity to "get it right" on the first try, people are less able to learn during the process and ultimately get it right. Any implementation process that involves uncertainty is most successful when participants are open to change, eager to find the best fit, and recognize that other people may have different perspectives. When people are very aware that others may have observed or interpreted something in a different way, they are more likely to be curious and to engage each other in relevant discussions about what to try. This is the very essence of a learning frame. To even consider this possibility, however, requires either an innate or trained habit of being self-aware, collaborative, and curious. Unfortunately, these traits and their corresponding cognitive frame rarely appear spontaneously in corporate and other organizational settings.

Changing Frames

In general, researchers agree that many of the spontaneous frames we bring to work are inherently about self-protection. Unfortunately, protection comes at a cost. Self-protective frames dramatically inhibit the opportunity to learn and improve. Research shows that people can learn to reframe and shift from spontaneous self-protective frames to reflective or learning-oriented frames. When this happens, the new frames are no longer tacit—at least not at first—but rather explicitly imposed on a situation or project in an effort to be effective. Following are steps for developing and reinforcing a learning frame, along with specific tactics to help individuals embrace a new way of interpreting their roles.

Establishing a Learning Frame

In successful organizations that adopted learning frames, the collective learning process consisted of four tightly coupled, recurring steps. The first step was enrollment of carefully selected team members by the leader, followed by team preparation, and then by multiple cycles of trial and reflection. Table 7.2 summarizes these steps and shows specific activities that successful implementers of the new technology had in common. It also suggests underlying cognitions supportive of these activities.

Table 7.2 Activities and Cognitive Frames for Successful Implementation

Step	Activities	Frames (Implicit Cognitions)	Effects
Enrollment	Communicate deliberateness in project team selection. Communicate purpose of project.	The project will create significant change in this organization or in people's jobs. Others play an important role in whether or not it succeeds.	Participants feel part of a team, have a shared sense of purpose, and feel committed to the project.

Table 7.2 *(continued)*

Step	Activities	Frames (Implicit Cognitions)	Effects
Preparation	Offline sessions to safely explore implications of the new technology or other change. Practice with new behaviors.	We need to learn how to work together and to anticipate problems if the project is going to succeed.	Participants develop an increasing willingness to take interpersonal risks in the project team and are motivated to expend effort on novel and uncertain actions.
Trial	Try out new concepts, processes, and tools. Pay close attention to what happens.	Actions at this stage of implementation are experiments. It's not about getting it right the first time. I feel a sense of curiosity about what will happen.	Every event, every action is seen as an opportunity to learn; people pay attention and are alert for possible changes that could be made.

(continued)

Table 7.2 (*continued*)

Step	Activities	Frames (Implicit Cognitions)	Effects
Reflection	Discuss trial results.	It will help me/us to learn from the past trials. I wonder what others may have seen that I missed.	Participants discuss what they did and what happened. Then they analyze what it means and brainstorm alternatives if needed.

Enrollment

A critical feature of enrollment is communicating to others that they are being specifically selected for a project or role. This builds intellectual and emotional commitment to the work. Enrollment is also about building awareness that a new technology imposes change, that change is challenging, and that everyone involved will affect whether or not the change succeeds. Enrollment, which is a fundamental leadership action, sets the tone of the journey that follows. It may be the first communication about a proposed change, enabling team members to form first impressions about what lies ahead for them and for the organization. When first impressions contain excitement or confidence that one's participation matters to outcomes, it can have a lasting effect.

Preparation

Preparation may involve attendance at an off-site training, or in-house team practice sessions, or it may be a quick team-building meeting to get to know others' strengths, weaknesses, hopes, and fears. Depending on the nature of the project, preparation sessions should include discussion of how existing routines may need to be altered in order to collect ideas for getting this to happen. More important, having an explicit practice session reduces the real and perceived risks of trying new things in "real" situations where customers or other outsiders could be harmed or receive a negative impression. Practice also enables team members to refine their own skills and integrate their actions with those of other participants. Other activities that should take place during the preparation phase include the establishment of team norms, a thorough discussion of how the team should work together, how to encourage speaking up with concerns and observations, and how power relations might affect the group.

Trial

The next step in the team learning process is a first, real trial of the new technology or other change. This means doing actual work while actively framing that work as an experiment from which much may be learned. In the trial step, people will begin to envision and enact how the new process or technology transforms the way work is done in the organization. The goal here is not to execute perfectly on the first try, but rather to quickly identify what adjustments or changes may be necessary for future success. Trials work well when those involved are curious and inquisitive.

Reflection

Paired with the previous step, reflection constitutes an opportunity to learn from what worked and what failed. Salient observations should then be used to make potential improvements after each round of trials. Together, these last two steps, trial and reflection, are the basis of a learning cycle that fuels successful implementation or innovation. Until such time as a new process or technology is completely routine, each use of it is an experiment, and each may be subtly different from prior use. Such differences are only useful if they are noticed, analyzed for their impact, and considered in the design of the next trial. In this way, the design of subsequent action continuously benefits from the knowledge gained in the prior cycle. Change happens through iteration.

Reinforcing a Learning Frame

One factor that facilitates deeper acceptance of a learning frame is making its use public rather than practicing it privately. Whether leading or participating in implementation projects, individuals seeking to follow the tactics for reframing can be open with others about what they are trying to do—enabling others to understand, provide feedback about, and even experiment with the learning frame themselves. Note that this is not the typical way leaders act; more often, they keep their strategy for engaging others (even when noble) to themselves. Here are five leadership tactics for reinforcing a learning frame:

- Use verbal and visual discourse to promote the learning frame.

- Reinforce this framing by explaining and modeling the desired interpersonal and collaborative behaviors.

- Explain these desired behaviors in practical terms, such as "Speak up if you see something wrong" or "Just pick up the phone and ask if you have a question."

- Initiate activities, for example, a kick-off meeting, a meeting to identify personal goals within the teaming or learning effort, and training on how to efficiently deal with interpersonal conflict. These can facilitate new processes or routines and help team members build confidence.

- Use artifacts such as a prominent sign in the project work area to visually reinforce the learning frame.

The Ideal Employee?

This week has emphasized the use of deliberate framing. But it's the unconscious frames that may exert the strongest influence on learning in an organization. Many managers have a taken-for-granted concept of an ideal employee. Consider the following: an ideal employee can handle with ease any problem that comes along (without bothering managers, of course), quietly corrects errors (their own and others') without making a fuss, performs flawlessly, and is deeply committed to the organization and its processes. I often pose this hypothetical person to managers, and I ask, "What's wrong with this employee?" They nearly always respond, "They don't exist!" My response is, no, that's not the problem. They exist. Every large organization has a few of these tireless and unassuming souls. But that's not the real problem. What's wrong with this so-called ideal employee is that they are making it more difficult for the organization to learn.

In the learning organization, problems and errors must be reported so everyone can learn. Flawless performance means not stretching enough. And the organization's processes need to be challenged, not blindly followed and enforced. In reflecting on our study explaining why hospitals don't learn from failures, Anita Tucker and I suggested, provocatively, that managers who want to build a learning organization must reframe the ideal employee in their own minds—and get ready to celebrate the disruptive questioner who simply won't leave well enough alone. This organizational-learning enabler is constantly questioning and improving, not accepting and using, current practices.

Tactics for Individual Reframing

Until this point, framing has been discussed as a leaders' job. Indeed, framing is one of the most important ways leaders can positively influence others and shape outcomes. However, anyone involved in a change initiative, in any role, can exert leadership in the form of helping to establish or reinforce a learning frame. Facing significant change, formal leaders should not be the only ones to actively frame the work ahead as a collaborative learning journey. General participation in cocreating a learning mindset not only ensures that it is widely shared but also helps others build their own leadership skills.

Here are four tactics that anyone confronted with the challenge of teaming, learning, implementing new technology, or driving organizational change can use to help adjust an existing cognitive frame:

- Tell yourself that the project is different from anything you've done before and presents an exciting opportunity to try out new approaches and learn from them.

- See yourself as critical to a successful outcome and yet as unable to achieve success without the willing participation of others.

- Tell yourself that others are vitally important to a successful outcome and may provide key knowledge or suggestions that you can't anticipate in advance.

- Communicate with others exactly as you would if the preceding three statements were true.

Framing the Picture of Success

Framing helps people interpret change in a positive and productive light and facilitates understanding of new performance expectations. In this activity, we examine the power of framing to improve results.

Activity

Reflect on the following questions:

Can you think of a time that you've worked on a task with as aspirational purpose? How about one with a defensive purpose? Which one felt better and why?

_____

_____

_____

What does a leader see as their role in a learning frame? How does this differ from the leader's role in an execution frame?

_____

_____

_____

What makes for the "ideal employee" in most managers' minds? What explains this tacit belief? Do you agree that this type of employee is truly ideal? Why or why not?

_____

_____

_____

Working Without Fear

Benchmark goal: Create a fearless organization.

Whenever you are trying to get people on the same page, with common goals and a shared appreciation for what they're up against, you're setting the stage for psychological safety. The most important skill to master is that of framing the work. If near perfection is what is needed to satisfy demanding car customers, leaders must know to frame the work by alerting workers to catch and correct tiny deviations before the car proceeds down the assembly line. If zero worker fatalities in a dangerous platinum mine is the goal, leaders must frame physical safety as a worthy and challenging but attainable goal. If discovering new cures is the goal, leaders know to motivate researchers to generate smart hypotheses for experiments and to feel okay about being wrong far more often than right.

Setting the Stage for Psychological Safety

Leaders have a special responsibility for creating psychological safety for their teams, but they also have special tools for doing so. In this week, we look at the tools leaders have for creating an environment where team members feel psychologically safe, productive mistakes are allowed, people can speak their minds, and every employee understands they make a contribution. Table 8.1 is a summary of the leader's tool kit.

Table 8.1   The Leader's Tool Kit for Building Psychological Safety

Category	Setting the Stage	Inviting Participation	Responding Productively
Leadership tasks	**Frame the Work** • Set expectations about failure, uncertainty, and interdependence to clarify the need for voice. **Emphasize Purpose** • Identify what's at stake, why it matters, and for whom.	**Demonstrate Situational Humility** • Acknowledge gaps. **Practice Inquiry** • Ask good questions. • Model intense listening. **Set Up Structures and Processes** • Create forums for input. • Provide guidelines for discussion	**Express Appreciation** • Listen. • Acknowledge and thank. **Destigmatize Failure** • Look forward. • Offer help. • Discuss, consider, and brainstorm next steps. **Sanction Clear Violations**
Accomplishes	Shared expectations and meaning	Confidence that voice is welcome	Orientation toward continuous learning

Framing the Work

Because fear of (reporting) failure is such a key indicator of an environment with low levels of psychological safety, how leaders present the role of failure is essential. Astro Teller at Google X observed that "the only way to get people to work on big, risky things . . . is if you make that the path of least resistance for them [and] make it safe to fail." In other words, unless a leader expressly and actively makes it psychologically safe to do so, people will automatically seek to avoid failure. So how did Teller reframe failure to make it okay? By saying, believing, and convincing others that "I'm not pro failure, I'm pro learning."

Note that failure plays a different role in different kinds of work. In high-volume repetitive work, such as in an assembly plant, a fast-food restaurant, or even a kidney dialysis center, many failures are avoidable. Failing to correctly plug a patient into a dialysis machine or install an automobile airbag in precisely the right manner can have disastrous consequences. So in this kind of work it's vital that people eagerly catch and correct deviations from best practice. Here, celebrating failure is a matter of viewing such deviations as "good-catch" events and appreciating those who noticed tiny mistakes as observant contributors to the mission.

In innovation and research, however, little is known about how to obtain a desired result. Creating a movie, a line of original clothing, or a technology that can convert seawater to fuel are all examples. In this context, dramatic failures must be courted and celebrated because they are an integral part of the journey to success. Between these two extremes, where much of the work done today falls, are complex operations, such as hospitals or financial institutions. Here, vigilance and teamwork are both vital to preventing avoidable failures and celebrating intelligent ones.

Reframing failure starts with understanding types of failures:

- Basic failures (never good news)
- Complex failures (still not good news)
- Intelligent failures (not fun, but must be considered good news because of the value they bring)

Basic failures are deviations from recommended procedures that produce bad outcomes. If someone fails to don safety glasses in a factory and suffers an eye injury, this is a basic failure. Complex failures occur in familiar contexts when a confluence of factors come together in a way that may never have occurred before; consider the severe flooding of the Wall Street subway station in New York City during Superstorm Sandy in 2012. With vigilance, complex failures can sometimes, but not always, be avoided. Neither basic nor complex failures are worthy of celebration.

By contrast, intelligent failures, as the term implies, must be celebrated so as to encourage more of them. Intelligent failures, like the basic and complex, are still results no one wanted. But, unlike the other two categories, they are the result of a thoughtful foray into new territory. An important part of framing is making sure people understand that failures will happen. Some failures are genuinely good news; some are not, but no matter what type they are, our primary goal is to learn from them.

Clarifying the Need for Voice

Framing the work also involves calling attention to other ways, beyond failure's prevalence, in which tasks and environments differ. Three especially important dimensions are uncertainty, interdependence, and what's at stake—all of which also have implications for failure (e.g. expectations about its frequency, its value, and its consequences). Emphasizing uncertainty reminds people that they need to be curious and alert to pick up early indicators of change in, say, customer preferences in a new market, a patient's reaction to a drug, or new technologies on the horizon.

Emphasizing interdependence lets people know that they're responsible for understanding how their tasks interact with other people's tasks. Interdependence encourages frequent conversations to figure out the impact their work is having on others and to convey in turn the impact others' work has on them. Interdependent work requires communication. In other words, when leaders frame the work, they are emphasizing the need for taking interpersonal risks like sharing ideas and concerns.

Finally, clarifying the stakes is important whether the stakes are high or low. Reminding people that human life is on the line—say, in a hospital, a mine, or at NASA—helps put interpersonal risk in perspective. People are more likely to speak up—thereby overcoming the inherent asymmetry of voice and silence—if leaders frame its importance. Similarly, reminding people that the only thing that is at stake is a bruised ego when a lab experiment doesn't go as hoped is a good way to get them to be willing to go for it—offer possibly crazy ideas and figure out which ones to test first!

Finally, how most people see bosses presents a crucial area for reframing. As a default, bosses are viewed as having answers, being able to give orders, and being positioned to assess whether the orders are well executed. With this frame, others are merely subordinates expected to do as they are told. The default set of frames makes interpersonal fear sensible.

In a world in which bosses have the answers and absolute authority over how your work is judged, it makes sense to fear the boss and to think very carefully about what you reveal. The reframe, by contrast, spells out logic that clarifies the necessity for a psychologically safe environment. This logic applies to the successful execution of work in most organizations today.

The reframe shows that leaders must establish and cultivate psychological safety to succeed in most work environments today. The leader is obliged to set direction for the work, to invite relevant input to clarify and improve on the general direction that has been set, and to create conditions for continued learning to achieve excellence.

In the reframe, those who are not the boss are seen as valued contributors—that is, as people with crucial knowledge and insight. When a leader asks people to speak up about patient error or orchestrates staff meetings to give everyone a chance to speak, they do so because it will improve decision-making and execution—not because they want to be nice. Leaders in a volatile, uncertain, complex, and ambiguous (VUCA) world, who understand that today's work requires continuous learning to figure out when and how to change course, must consciously reframe how they think, from the default frames that we all bring to work unconsciously to a more productive reframe.

Framing the work is not something that leaders do once, and then it's done. Framing is ongoing. Frequently calling attention to levels of uncertainty or interdependence helps people remember that they must be alert and candid to perform well.

Emphasizing Purpose

Emphasizing a sense of purpose is another key element of setting the stage for psychological safety. Motivating people by articulating a compelling purpose is a well-established leadership task. Leaders who remind people of why what they do matters—for customers, for the world—help create the energy that carries them through challenging moments. Note that even when it seems obvious (for instance, taking care of vulnerable patients) that the work is meaningful, leaders still must take the time to emphasize the purpose the organization serves. This is because anyone can get tired, distracted, and frustrated and lose sight of the larger picture of what's at stake.

Meaning can be defined and framed in other ways, too. Most leaders would be well served by stopping to reflect on the purpose that motivates them and makes the organization's work meaningful to the broader community. Having done so, they should ask themselves how often and how vigorously they are conveying this compelling rationale for the work to others. Our primal need to feel purpose and meaning in our lives, including at work, has been demonstrated by numerous studies in psychology.

Inviting Participation So People Respond

The second essential activity in the leaders' tool kit is inviting participation in a way that people find compelling and genuine. The goal is to lower what is usually a too-high bar for what's considered appropriate participation. Realizing that self-protection is natural, the invitation to participate must be crystal clear if people are going to choose to engage rather than to play it safe. Two essential behaviors that signal an invitation is genuine are adopting a mindset of situational humility and engaging in proactive inquiry. Designing structures for input, another powerful tool I discuss in this section, also serves as an invitation for voice.

Situational Humility

The bottom line is that no one wants to take the interpersonal risk of imposing ideas when the boss appears to think they know everything. A learning mindset, which blends humility and curiosity, mitigates this risk. A learning mindset recognizes that there is always more to learn.

Frankly, adopting a humble mindset when faced with the complex, dynamic, uncertain world in which we all work today is simply realism. The term *situational humility* captures this concept well (the need for humility lies in the situation) and may make it easier for leaders, especially those with abundant self-confidence, to recognize the validity, and the power, of a humble mindset. MIT Professor Ed Schein calls this *here-and-now humility.* Keep in mind that confidence and humility are not opposites. Confidence in one's abilities and knowledge, when warranted, is far preferable to false modesty. But humility is not modesty, false or otherwise. Humility is the simple recognition that you don't have all the answers, and you certainly don't have a crystal ball. Research shows that when leaders express humility, teams engage in more learning behavior.

In our study of neonatal intensive care units, Ingrid Nembhard, Anita Tucker, and I found that neonatal intensive care units with high psychological safety had substantially better results from their quality improvement work than those with low psychological safety. A factor we called *leadership inclusiveness* made the difference.

Building on this work, Israeli researchers Reuven Hirak and Abraham Carmeli and two of their colleagues surveyed employees from clinical units in a large hospital in Israel on leader inclusiveness, psychological safety, units' ability to learn from failures, and unit performance. They found that units in which leaders were perceived as more inclusive had higher psychological safety, which led to increased learning from failure and better unit performance. In sum, leaders who are approachable and accessible, acknowledge their fallibility, and proactively invite input from others can do much to establish and enhance psychological safety in their organizations. Powerful tools, indeed.

Practice Proactive Inquiry

The second tool for inviting participation is inquiry. Inquiry is purposeful probing to learn more about an issue, situation, or person. The foundational skill lies in cultivating genuine interest in others' responses. Why is this hard? Because all adults, especially high-achieving ones, are subject to a cognitive bias called *naïve realism*, which gives us the experience of "knowing" what's going on. We believe we are seeing "reality," rather than a subjective view of reality. As a result, we often fail to wonder what others are seeing. We fail to be curious.

Worse, many leaders, even when they are motivated to ask a question, worry that it will make them look uninformed or weak. Further exacerbating the challenge, some companies sport "a culture of telling," as a senior executive in a global pharmaceutical company put it in a recent conversation we had about his company. In a culture of telling, asking gets short shrift. Yet when leaders overcome these biases to ask genuine questions, it fosters psychological safety. Contrary to what many may believe, asking questions tends to make the leader seem not weak but thoughtful and wise.

All of us can benefit from introducing more inquiry into our work. The essential skill of inquiry involves picking the right type of question for a situation. For instance, questions can go broad or deep. To broaden understanding of a situation or expand an option set, ask, "what might we be missing?", "what other ideas could we generate?", or "who has a different perspective?" Such questions ensure that more comprehensive information is considered and that a larger set of options is generated related to a problem or decision. Other questions are designed to deepen understanding. Ask, "what leads you to think so?" or "can you give me an example?" Such questions are crucial to helping people learn about each other's expertise and goals. Moreover, when asked thoughtfully, a good question indicates to others that their voices are desired—instantly making that moment psychologically safe for offering a response.

Designing Structures for Input

A third way to invite participation and reinforce psychological safety is to implement structures designed to elicit employee input. One way to chip away at interpersonal fear is through employee-to-employee learning structures, as Google has done with its creation of the "g2g" (Googler-to-Googler) network, consisting of more than 6,000 Google employees who volunteer time to helping their peers learn. Participants in g2g do one-on-one mentoring, coach teams on psychological safety, and teach courses in professional skills ranging from leadership to Python coding. Google claims that g2g has helped develop the skills of countless employees. It is also helping to build a psychologically safe culture where everyone is both a learner and a teacher.

The global food company Groupe Danone created structured conference events called *knowledge marketplaces* to foster inquiry and knowledge sharing across country business units. Although many good ideas and practices that improved operational performance came out of these workshops, the executives who sponsored them saw the most important outcome as a shift in the organizational culture toward speaking up, asking for help, and sharing good ideas.

Responding Productively to Voice—No Matter Its Quality

To reinforce a climate of psychological safety, it's imperative that leaders—at all levels—respond productively to the risks people take.

Productive responses are characterized by three elements: expressions of appreciation, destigmatizing failure, and sanctioning clear violations.

Express Appreciation

Stanford Professor Carol Dweck, whose celebrated research on mindset shows the power of a learning orientation for individual achievement and resilience in the face of challenge, notes the importance of praising people for efforts, regardless of the outcome. When people believe their performance is an indication of their ability or intelligence, they are less likely to take risks for fear of a result that would disconfirm their ability. But when people believe that performance reflects effort and good strategy, they are eager to try new things and willing to persevere despite adversity and failure.

Praising effort is especially important in uncertain environments, where good outcomes are not always the result of good process, and vice versa. Although CEOs should take the lead in praising effort, an equally important leadership responsibility for C-suite-level executives is making sure that people throughout the organization respond productively to their colleagues. It helps if everyone understands the logic conveyed in Figure 8.1, which depicts the imperfect relationship between process and outcome.

Clearly, good process can lead to good outcomes, and bad process can lead to bad outcomes. But, good process also can produce bad outcomes (especially facing high uncertainty or complexity, as in VUCA conditions), and bad process can produce a good outcome (when you get lucky) or the illusion of a good outcome. The lack of simple cause-effect relationships in uncertain, ambiguous environments reinforces the importance of productive responses to outcomes of all kinds, but especially to bad news outcomes.

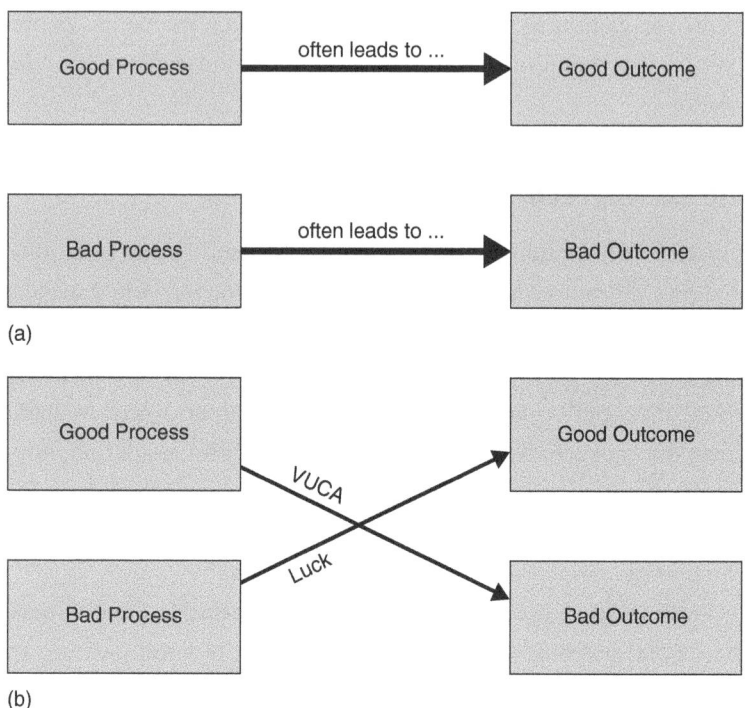

Figure 8.1 The imperfect relationship between process and outcome.

Productive responses often include expressions of appreciation, ranging from the small ("thank you so much for speaking up") to the elaborate—celebrations or bonuses in response to intelligent failure.

Destigmatize Failure

Failure is a necessary part of uncertainty and innovation, but this must be made clear to reinforce the invitation for voice. Leaders who respond to all failures in the same way will not create a healthy environment for learning. When a failure occurs because someone violated a rule or value that matters in the organization, this is very different than when a thoughtful hypothesis in the lab turns out to be wrong. Although obvious in concept, in practice people routinely get this wrong.

A productive response to *intelligent* failure can mean actually celebrating the news. Some years ago, the chief scientific officer at Eli Lilly introduced "failure parties" to honor intelligent, high-quality scientific experiments that failed to achieve the desired results. Might this be a bridge too far? I don't think so. First, and most obvious, it helps build a psychologically safe climate for thoughtful risks, which is mission critical in science. Second, it helps people acknowledge failures in a timely way, which allows redeployment of valuable resources—scientists and materials—to new projects earlier rather than later, potentially saving thousands of dollars. Third, when you hold a party, people tend to show up—which means they learn about the failure. This in turn lowers the risk that the company will repeat the same failure. An intelligent failure the first time around no longer qualifies as intelligent the second time.

In brief, a productive response to basic failures is to double down on prevention, usually a combination of training and improved system design to make it easier for people to do the right thing. However, there are instances in which a basic failure is the result of a blameworthy action or a repeated instance of deviation from prescribed process, impervious to prior attempts at redirection. In such cases, usually rare, there is an obligation to act in ways that prevent future occurrence. This may mean fines or other sanctions, and in some cases even firing someone.

Sanction Clear Violations

Yes, firing can sometimes be an appropriate and productive response—to a blameworthy act. But won't this kill the psychological safety? No. Most people are thoughtful enough to recognize (and appreciate) that when people violate rules or repeatedly take risky shortcuts, they are putting themselves, their colleagues, and their organization at risk. In short, psychological safety is reinforced rather than harmed by fair, thoughtful responses to potentially dangerous, harmful, or sloppy behavior.

In July 2017, Google engineer James Damore wrote a 10-page memo railing against the company's diversity stance, arguing that biological differences explained why Google had fewer women engineers and paid them less well than men, and circulated it widely within the company. Someone then leaked the memo, creating a public firestorm.

How did Google respond? Damore was promptly and publicly fired a month later, earning the company both praise and criticism. Thoughtful arguments have been made on both sides of the firing debate. Rather than coming out on one side or the other, let's step back to consider when firing constitutes a "productive response," and when it doesn't.

Take this specific case. To begin, it is a shame that Damore chose to share his personal concerns electronically and widely within the company, all but ensuring that someone who disliked the memo would share it publicly. But once the inflammatory memo has been made public, how should a company respond? My intention is not to illuminate the specifics of Damore's memo at Google but rather to suggest a general strategy for productive responses to actions or events in your organization that you wish had not occurred.

If there are clear policies against the use of company email addresses or social media platforms for the expression of personal opinions, an employee who violates these policies commits what we can call a *blameworthy* act. In this case, a productive response indeed involves tough sanctions, which may include terminating the employee. A tough response is productive because it lets people know that the company is serious about its policies and values, which shapes future behavior, and because it constitutes a fair response to a stated violation.

If policies are unclear, however, a productive response is one that turns the unfortunate event into a different kind of learning opportunity—for the company and sometimes for the interested public. In the Damore case, executives might express dismay at the employee's opinion (and perhaps dismay at his ignorance of a larger set of societal forces that have systematically diminished advancement opportunities for certain demographic groups over decades). They might then go on to explain their plans for educating employees on what they believe to be the value of a diverse workforce.

In short, a productive response is concerned with future impact. Punishment sends a powerful message, and an appropriate one if boundaries were clear in advance. Indeed, it is vital to send messages that reinforce values the company holds dear. However, it is equally vital not to inadvertently send a message that says, "diverse opinions simply won't be tolerated here" or "one strike and you're out." Such messages reduce psychological safety and ultimately erode the quality of the work. By contrast, a message that reinforces the values and practices of a learning organization is, "it's okay to make a mistake, and it's okay to hold an opinion that others don't like, so long as you are willing to learn from the consequences." The most important goal is figuring out a way to help the organization learn from what happened.

Using the Leadership Tool Kit

Leaders have special responsibilities to create psychological safety on their teams, but they also have special tools. In this activity, you will reflect on the leader's tool kit for creating a psychologically safe team.

Activity

Reflect on the following questions:

What are the three types of failure? Do you agree that some types of failure are more productive (and therefore permissible, and even necessary) than others?

_____

_____

_____

Have you ever worked for a manager who avoided the top-down approach? One who actively sought opinions of team members and saw them as valuable contributors? Did it increase your psychological safety? Did it make you more willing to express opinions and admit errors?

_____

_____

_____

Is a firing ever a correct response to an employee expressing an opinion, even one that violates the company's values? Why or why not?

_____

_____

_____

Wrap-Up

Performance goal: Team fearlessly with psychological safety.

Psychological safety is not immunity from consequences, nor is it a state of high self-regard. In psychologically safe workplaces, people know they might fail, they might receive performance feedback that says they're not meeting expectations, and they might lose their jobs due to changes in the industry environment or even to a lack of competence in their role.

But in a psychologically safe workplace, people are not hindered by interpersonal fear. They feel willing and able to take the inherent interpersonal risks of candor.

Questions

1. Twenty-five years of research on psychological safety finds positive benefits for learning, engagement, and performance in a wide range of organizations. Have you worked in an environment where you felt psychologically safe? How did it compare to those where you did not?

2. Creating an environment that values employees yields benefits in engagement, problem-solving, and performance. Why do you think so many organizations create environments where employees don't feel valued?

Activity

For this activity, get a paper and pen to write answers to these prompts.

A lack of psychological safety can create an illusion of success that eventually turns into a serious business failure. Can you think of an example (from your own career or from the news) of a time when an illusion of success was created by fear of speaking out about failure? Do you think things would have been different if employees felt able to speak up?

A culture of silence (where team members are encouraged to keep secrets and cover up problems) is a dangerous culture. It can result in business failures, unnecessary costs, high employee turnover, legal trouble, and even a loss of life in some circumstances. Have you experienced a culture of silence in your career? Did negative consequences come from it?

Days 61–90

Performance goal: Innovate with teaming.

Consider Part III a road map for leaders who wish to inspire or participate in the innovation journey. Each of the following weeks covers one of four overarching recommendations for leaders seeking to enhance innovation in their organization: aim well, team up, fail well, and learn fast.

The following table summarizes the goals you will reflect on over the next 30 days. To keep yourself motivated, consider your personal goals and vision for success. What does innovation mean to you?

	Days 61–90
	Performance Goal: Innovate with teaming.
Week 9	**Benchmark Goal: Aim high: Discover how to choose a worthy goal.** • Do you agree that to innovate you need a worthy goal? • How does aiming high help to motivate a team? • Have you ever had a stretch goal that challenged you beyond what seemed feasible? How did you stay motivated?

	Days 61–90 **Performance Goal:** Innovate with teaming.
Week 10	**Benchmark Goal: Team up: Learn the keys to teaming up for innovation.** • Have you ever teamed up with "strange bedfellows" to achieve a challenging goal? How did it work out? • Do you agree that psychological safety is a must for teaming? • How do process guidelines contribute to effective teaming?
Week 11	**Benchmark Goal: Fail well: See how failure sets the stage for success.** • Do you agree that failure is a prerequisite of innovation? • Have you ever experienced a "good failure" in your career? • What did you learn from it? • Why is it important to "fail at the right scale"?
Week 12	**Benchmark Goal: Learn fast: Make the most of your failure.** • What are the four steps to learning fast? Which do you think is more important? • What are some of the barriers to learning? • Can you think of when you've struggled with those barriers?
Personal Goals and Vision for Success	
What do you hope to achieve by leveling up?	
How could your life change by reaching these goals?	

90 Days to Level Up Your Teamwork

Shooting for the Moon

Benchmark goal: Aim high: Discover how to choose a worthy goal.

Leaders seeking to inspire, enhance, or revive innovation in their organization often wonder what to do. They understand that just asking for innovation will not produce it. They recognize that cross-disciplinary groups do not always come up with terrific new ideas, and synergy is not a necessary outcome of collaboration across boundaries. In fact, without an unusual mix of openness, humility, talent, drive, and creativity, innovation may not occur. It is clear that leadership is needed to nurture these qualities in fluid groupings of people—often both inside and outside the organization—and channel them toward desired ends.

Teaming for innovation is dynamic. It involves identifying (often temporary) collaborators and getting up to speed quickly on what needs to be done and what role each collaborator can play. This kind of flexibility is needed more and more in workplaces across many industries. A growing portion of the work itself—whether product design, patient care, custom software, or strategic decision-making—presents complicated interdependencies that often have to be managed on the fly.

But no matter how flexible and willing one's colleagues may be, effective teaming rarely happens spontaneously. It takes effort. Teaming requires letting down your guard to work interdependently with others. It requires offering your ideas and skills thoughtfully while being equally, if not more, interested in what others have to offer, no matter what their status or position in the hierarchy. It requires accepting that it's simply not possible to look good or be right all the time. Teaming to innovate requires creativity, humility, empathy, and drive. Because these attributes can wax and wane in the real world, especially in the workplace, leaders need to nurture them.

In a nutshell, the leadership task in innovation is to keep people focused on what's at stake—on the purpose the organization seeks to serve and the goals it's striving to achieve—and to be stewards of the contradictory and paradoxical culture of innovation.

Consider this month a road map for leaders who wish to inspire or participate in the innovation journey. Each of the next four weeks look at four overarching recommendations for leaders seeking to enhance innovation in their organization:

- Aim high (this week)
- Team up (week 10)
- Fail well (week 11)
- Learn fast (week 12)

That's basically it. It's simple. (Note that simple doesn't mean easy!) And there is a final recommendation as well: repeat!

Innovation starts with a worthy aspiration. Although invention may occasionally occur as a result of pure brilliance, ingenuity, or the sheer pleasure of discovery, innovation is the result of an effortful and disciplined process. Effort and discipline thrive when people are motivated to strive for something more. Driven by a desire to do something new and useful, people are able and willing to take the risks that innovation entails. So, to foster innovation in your organization, start with some soul searching to identify a worthy aspiration—one that in some small way relates to creating a better world. Whether to create a brand-new product, service, or solution or merely a substantially better way of doing something we already do, innovation begins as a glimmer. An idea. Aiming high for a worthy goal, no matter how distant, engages and motivates people by involving them in something larger than themselves.

Of course, it's possible to innovate without worthy goals or lofty aims, but if you're interested in engaging smart, motivated people in the uncertain journey of innovation, a worthy aspiration is a valuable source of fuel.

Aiming High for Innovation

On August 5, 2010, more than half a million tons of rock collapsed in the San José copper mine in Northern Chile, completely blocking the entrance. Mining accidents are unfortunately common. But this one was unprecedented for several reasons: the distance of the miners from the surface, the sheer number of miners trapped, and the hardness of the rock, to name just a few. Thirty-three men were buried alive, under 2,000 feet of rock harder than granite. In Chile, initial estimates of the possibility of finding anyone alive were put at 10 percent—odds that diminished sharply two days later when rescue workers narrowly escaped a secondary collapse of the ventilation shaft, which permanently shut down the option of rescuing the miners through that route.

Yet within 70 days all 33 miners would be rescued. This extraordinary result occurred because several leaders committed to the aspirational goal of a successful rescue, despite the brutal odds against their success. That the rescue required innovation is self-evident—there simply was no existing solution, either inside or outside the mining industry, at the outset. It took the collaborative efforts of over 100 experts in diverse fields innovating to develop and execute a novel solution on the fly.

Innovation occurred in at least two very separate arenas. First, and most painful to consider, were the miners facing the challenge of physical and psychological survival. Innovation here took the form of a new social system—designed to maintain the life and sanity of 33 trapped men in dire circumstances. Second, a network of engineers and geologists came together from multiple organizations and nations to work on the technical problems of locating, reaching, and extracting the trapped miners. Their innovation produced the design and development of a completely novel rescue system. To support the actions of those above and below ground at the San José site, senior leaders in the Chilean government, including the nation's president, made decisions and provided resources and inspiration.

Teaming to Survive

Below ground, amidst shock and fear, leadership and teaming took shape after a tumultuous beginning. Immediately after the collapse, the miners scrambled to safety in the mine's small refuge. Luis Urzúa, who had formal leadership over the group as the shift supervisor, started by checking provisions in the refuge. Calmly and quickly, he focused on crucial survival needs, especially the limited available food (roughly the amount of food two miners would eat over 10 days). However, calm did not prevail. Mario Sepulveda, a charismatic 39-year old, outraged at the state of the mine and the company's long-standing lack of attention to safety, reacted angrily to the collapse. His energy attracted followers; factions and conflict soon emerged. Some wanted to take action of any kind to reach the outside world rather than sitting helplessly to await rescue. Others wanted to follow Urzúa's guidance. By the end of their first 24 hours, the miners were exhausted by failed attempts to communicate with the outside world and disoriented by the lack of natural light. With scant attention to sanitation or order and subdued by hunger and fatigue, they attempted to sleep.

On the second day, miner José Henríquez stepped in to urge the group to start each day with a collective prayer. Soon this became a sustaining routine and helped unite the group around a shared goal: survival. With no blueprint for how to survive in these conditions, conversation and experimentation were essential to discovering a way forward. In the days that followed, facing darkness, hunger, depression, filth, and illness, the miners cooperated intensely to maintain order, health, sanitation, and sanity.

Teaming to Solve Complex Technical Problems

Above ground, the Chilean Carabineros Special Operations Group—an elite police unit for rescue operations—arrived a few hours after the first collapse. Their initial attempt at rescue led to the ventilation shaft collapse, the rescue effort's dismal first failure. As news of a mine cave-in spread, family members, emergency response teams, rescue workers, and reporters also flooded to the site. Meanwhile, others in the Chilean mining community dispatched experts, drilling machines, and bulldozers. Codelco, the state-owned company overseeing the San José mine, sent Andre Sougarret, an engineer and manager with over 20 years of experience in mining who was known for his composure and ease with people, to lead the operation. Working with numerous other technical experts, Sougarret formed three teams to oversee different aspects of the operation. One team searched for the men, poking drill holes deep into the earth in the hopes of hearing sounds indicating that the men were alive. Another worked on how to keep them alive if found, and a third worked on how to extract them safely from the refuge. On October 13, miners began to be brought up, one by one, on a 15-minute journey to the surface. Over the next two days, they were hauled up, one after another, in the 28-inchwide escape capsule painted with the red, white, and blue of the Chilean flag. After a few minutes to hug relatives, each miner was taken for medical evaluation.

Neither Top-Down nor Bottom-Up

Reflecting on the Chilean rescue, it is clear that a top-down, command-and-control approach—the kind that can be successfully used in a crisis with a known solution, such as when a large fire breaks out or when an impending hurricane is detected—would have failed utterly. No one person, or even one leadership team, could have figured out how to solve this problem. It's also clear that simply encouraging everyone to try anything they wanted would have produced only chaos and harm. Family members, miners, and others with good intentions had to be held back numerous times from rushing headlong at the rock with pickaxes. Instead, what was required, facing the unprecedented scale of the disaster, was coordinated but flexible teaming—multiple temporary groups of people working separately on different types of problems and coordinating across groups, as needed. Such groups innovate in ways no one can anticipate at the outset. Doing this well involves progressive experimentation, a core discipline of innovation.

Aiming High with Meaning

What drives the hard and interpersonally challenging work of teaming for innovation? Let's face it; it's not easy to get up in the morning and come to work knowing you might fail several times before lunch! The hard intellectual and emotional work of innovation is fueled by a compelling purpose that addresses questions like, Why care? Why bother? Why should I put aside the momentary comfort of relaxing in order to exert the effort and subject myself to the risks involved in coming up with new solutions to old problems?

Emotions play a role in generating creative ideas. Emotions spark new connections between disparate experiences. Emotions also motivate and provide a foundation to return to when the going gets tough. The most motivating goals are connected to the objectives and frustrations of today's work. This close connection makes tolerable the daily risks and suffering (big and small) in the demanding environment of innovation, where nothing is certain.

Soon after assuming the CEO role at Children's Hospital and Clinics in Minneapolis, Minnesota, Judith Morath assembled a team she called the Patient Safety Steering Committee (PSSC). The PSSC was a select group of key influencers who would help design and launch the "Patient Safety Initiative." To identify those having interest and passion, as well as to communicate with as many people in the hospital as possible, Morath delivered a series of presentations about medical errors, citing the then still unfamiliar fact that as many as 98,000 hospitalized patients in the United States were dying annually from medical errors—more than the number from car accidents, breast cancer, or AIDS. The PSSC was deliberately diverse, comprising doctors and nurses, department heads and frontline staff, union members and executives. It was a group that understood and represented the organization well.

Despite the pedigree of the PSSC and Morath's compelling delivery, many initially pushed back against the idea of a patient safety initiative, reluctant to believe that errors were a problem at Children's. They believed the national statistics but did not believe those numbers applied to Children's. When your work involves taking care of vulnerable children, it's enormously threatening to be told that you might be doing things that harm them. Quite naturally, they resisted Morath's efforts to promote innovation.

Tempting as it must have been to simply reiterate her message more forcefully (given that she understood that all hospitals, because of their operational complexity, were vulnerable to error), Morath did not try to argue the point. Instead, she thoughtfully responded to the resistance with inquiry. "Okay, this data may not be applicable here," she concurred. Then she probed gently, "Tell me, what was your own experience this week, in the units, with your patients? Was everything as safe as you would like it to have been?"

The Power of Inquiry

This simple inquiry seems to have transformed the dialogue. Note its features. Her question is an invitation, one that is genuine, curious, direct, and concrete. Each caregiver is invited to consider their own patients and experiences, in their own unit, over the prior few days. Moreover, the question is aspirational—not, "Did you see things that were unsafe?" but rather, "Was everything as safe as you would like it to have been?" It respects others' experience while it invites aspiration. Too many would-be leaders forget about the power of inquiry and instead rely on forceful advocacy to bring others along. As Morath showed, inquiry respects and invites. As people began to discuss with her and with others incidents they had thought were unique or idiosyncratic, they realized that most of their colleagues had experienced similar events. As Morath put it, "I found that most people had been at the center of a health care situation where something did not go well. They were quick to recognize that the hospital could be doing better." She led as many as 18 focus groups throughout the organization to enable people to air their concerns and ideas.

Making It Safe to Talk About Problems

To build the psychological safety needed for the inevitably difficult conversations about errors and failures, Morath frequently described her philosophy on patient safety to anyone who would listen. In her words, "Health care is a very complex system, and complex systems are, by their very nature, risk-prone. The culture of health care must be one of everyone working together to understand safety, identify risks, and report them without fear of blame. We must look at ways to change the whole system when we manage to zero defects." By emphasizing the systemic nature of failures, she sought to help people move away from a tendency to find and blame individual culprits.

Morath knew firsthand about the aftershock and emotional pain of medical accidents for health care workers. She never forgot one she'd witnessed 30 years earlier, when she was a young nurse: a four-year-old patient died from an anesthesia error. What Morath remembered, even more than the devastation of the child's death, was that "the nurse who felt responsible 'went home that day and never returned,' giving up the career she loved due to a profound and crushing feeling of guilt. Doctors and other nurses 'just shut down' and never talked to one another about what happened. The hospital's attorneys swooped in to do damage control. 'It just didn't sit right and it plagued me,'" Morath said decades later.

So she introduced a new system for reporting medical incidents called *blameless reporting*. The idea was to allow people to communicate confidentially or anonymously about medical accidents without being punished for doing so, so as to bring as many of these problems as possible to light, to determine their underlying causes, and to keep caring professionals in their positions.

Morath also instituted new words—new ways of talking about safety lapses that would be less emotionally threatening. For example, she encouraged people to substitute *study* for *investigation*. To Morath, study meant a way of learning how systems work and how the pieces fit together. An investigation, however, was more like a police lineup, assigning blame to someone in a linear search to determine a single cause. By avoiding words that implied blame and encouraging language conducive to learning from failures, Morath was trying to make it psychologically safe to talk about error.

Just as important, she believed that the whole meaning of *error* had to be reframed. She explained to people that in hospitals, *accidents* (a term preferable to *error*) arose from faulty systems rather than faulty persons. Complex systems are failure-prone; individual clinicians involved in a system failure are victims of that complexity, just like their patients.

Last, *blame* was to be replaced by the word *accountable*, defined as being responsible for the duties of a particular job and whatever knowledge it required, as well as for understanding the larger system in which one was a human component. All of these linguistic interventions were designed to make it safe to engage in the interpersonally risky behaviors of innovation.

When leaders successfully engage employees in an innovation process, ideas start to bubble up, experiments start to happen, and activities start to take hold and spread. To a manager seeking to "get the job done," the process might at first seem laborious and slow. But engaging people as active thinkers and learners is the only way to innovate in a complex system like a hospital, where solutions simply don't exist at the outset.

It's a Stretch

On the innovation journey, aiming high means stretching beyond what seems initially feasible. The aspiration must be truly challenging.

At the same time, it's important that it not be completely implausible. The distinction can be a very fine line. The goal should inspire but not turn off or depress those who wish to innovate. Developing systems whereby patients are safe from medical mishap is one such goal. It's enormously challenging, but through innovative ways of changing the culture of reporting and by introducing better mechanisms for catching and correcting small process failures before they reach patients, it is not impossible to dramatically improve patient safety. Morath's innovation journey was both cultural and procedural.

Worthy Aspirations That Motivate Innovation

The opportunity to make a difference turns out to be a key driver of innovation. When people share an ambitious goal—together with a vision of a better future—it gives them a shared identity. It builds camaraderie.

What's so great about camaraderie? First, it makes work more fun. Second, people feel safer, and when people feel safer it's easier to be creative. And third, because innovation is heavy lifting, people must have confidence in each other's abilities. Envisioning a process or a product that has never existed requires conviction. For this reason, the goal, as noted, should be a stretch, but not absurd!

Finally, as any reader who has experienced true teamwork in the pursuit of innovation knows well, there's nothing better. At times, you believe that anything's possible when a group of dedicated people put their minds to doing what was thought to be impossible.

Innovation is a team sport. But teaming to innovate isn't always a smooth ride. Next, I explain why people must span boundaries, build psychological safety, and cool conflict to make teaming work and enable innovation to flourish.

Aiming High and True

If you're interested in engaging smart, motivated people in the uncertain journey of innovation, a worthy aspiration is a valuable source of fuel. In this activity, you examine the role of a laudable goal in spurring innovation.

Activity

Reflect on the following questions:

Have you ever been a part of a team working on a challenge that deeply mattered (to you or someone else)? How did it affect your approach?

_____

_____

_____

Do you agree that emotion plays an important role in innovation? Why or why not?

_____

_____

_____

How important is it to you to feel camaraderie with your team? Do you believe it's possible to be a part of an effective team if there is no camaraderie? Explain your answer.

_____

_____

_____

Coming Together

Benchmark goal: Team up: Learn the keys to teaming up for innovation.

Like it or not, innovation is a team sport. Few worthy innovations are accomplished alone or even by groups of people who have the same basic knowledge and expertise. This week I look at the second key factor for innovation: teaming up. I look at what it takes to team and explain why teaming is more challenging than it might first appear. I explore the crucial role of psychological safety—along with other enabling factors—in helping people team effectively. And because teaming across disciplinary lines is so vital to innovation, I pay particular attention to the types of boundaries people confront when teaming to innovate and how to bridge them effectively.

Sometimes a Team Calls for Strange Bedfellows

It is hard to imagine two more different thought worlds than Hollywood and the CIA. But what makes the story of the fate of six American hostages in Iran truly gripping is the teaming between these strange bedfellows and how it brought the hostages home. As you read this story, consider the types of boundaries between these players, the nature of the teaming that occurred, and the innovative solution itself. How did teaming up across boundaries produce innovation?

Early in the morning of November 4, 1979, at the United States Embassy in Tehran, Iran's capital city, a rapidly growing crowd of anti-American student protestors was demanding that ousted monarch (Shah) Mohammad Reza Pahlavi be returned from US exile. They wanted him to be tried by the revolutionary government led by Ayatollah Khomeini. The crowd rushed the embassy gates, chanting, "Allahu Akbar!" (God is great!) and "Marg bar Amrika!" (Death to America!). Soon students were scaling the walls of the embassy. Within minutes, the protestors swarmed the vast compound that contained the ambassador's residence and staff offices.

Consular diplomat Martin Lijek, in Iran on his first consular post, hoped the adjacent visa-processing building where he worked would not be in the protestors' path. He hoped that no one would suspect that a small collection of American embassy staff, Iranian employees, and visa applicants was on the second floor. Martin's group included his wife, Cora (consular assistant), Joseph Stafford (senior foreign service officer), Stafford's wife, Kathleen (consular assistant), and Robert Anders (senior consular officer).

Suddenly, the building went dark as power was cut. Gunshots rang out in the compound. Escaping capture was paramount: Iranian employees had known neighbors who were apprehended and executed by revolutionary guards. As the crowd neared their building, Martin and his peers destroyed the plates used to make visa stamps, improvised an evacuation plan, and ushered both staff and applicants to the back door. This was the sole exit on the embassy compound with direct street access.

The Iranian visa applicants exited first, in small groups, ahead of the American staff. One Iranian group was captured moments later and taken back to the embassy. The Lijeks, Staffords, and Anders headed to the British Embassy, several blocks away. The American escapees had almost reached the embassy when they encountered another demonstration.

Eventually, the group found refuge in the residence of Ken Taylor, the Canadian ambassador. The six became known at the State Department and CIA as the "houseguests." Aware that the lives of the Canadian ambassador and his so-called houseguests were at risk if the presence of the Americans became known, experts in Washington, DC, were considering a number of rescue plans, mostly involving overland routes bypassing roads and checkpoints.

Tony Mendez, Graphics Authentication Division head at the CIA, was called in to come up with a plan for bringing the hostages home. False identities were Mendez's specialty. He had spent 14 years in the CIA's Office of Technical Service—a real-world version of James Bond's "Q" branch—and had helped more than 100 agents and others escape life-threatening situations abroad.

The problem was that neither the Canadian nor American diplomatic corps leaders could conceive of a credible reason for any North Americans to be in Tehran after the hostage crisis had begun. Teachers, agricultural researchers, and others had all left. In the midst of the brainstorming, Mendez had a unique idea: to assemble a film scouting crew.

The plan was fleshed out as follows. Mendez would play the role of fictitious film producer Kevin Harkins from Canada and request a "location scout" trip to Iran for a Hollywood studio film. The concept seemed plausible because so-called Hollywood creative types might conceivably be oblivious to the situation in revolutionary Iran.

Focusing on finding the right backdrop for a new movie, perhaps a science fiction story in need of an exotic desert landscape, a Hollywood producer might just be crazy enough to scout out the view in Iran. Moreover, the Iranian government wanted the hard currency and might welcome this kind of business venture. A film production could mean millions of US dollars.

Pursuing this idea, Mendez needed partners. The cover story seemed plausible. But a great deal of work still needed to be done to fill in the details for an operation that could withstand scrutiny while manhunting Americans was in high gear. To prepare the foundation for this cover, Mendez flew to Los Angeles in mid-January to meet John Chambers, a veteran makeup artist who had won a 1969 Academy Award for *Planet of the Apes* and was also a longtime Mendez collaborator. Chambers invited makeup artist and special effects expert Bob Sidell to join the meeting.

Chambers found a well-suited script in the vast archives of submitted screenplays never filmed. Mendez gave the script a new title, *Argo*, the name of the vessel used by Greek mythology hero Jason (and his Argonauts) on his daring voyage across the world to retrieve the Golden Fleece. Mendez and Chambers designed a full-page ad for the film to run in key trade magazines *Variety* and the *Hollywood Reporter*.

Finally, Mendez obtained false Canadian passports for the six and flew to Tehran. Meeting the hostages, he explained the cover story and presented Jack Kirby's conceptual art, the screenplay, the ad in *Variety*, and the "Studio Six" business cards. With some reluctance, the houseguests agreed the ruse could work and set about memorizing their new identities to match their fake Canadian passports. Soon they were headed to the Tehran airport to make their dangerous escape from Iran—in plain sight.

After several tense moments at the gate, Mendez and his "film crew" boarded the plane. The plane took off, and Mendez and the six escapees breathed a collective sigh of relief. Together they had successfully accomplished the most creative and improbable "exfiltration" of Mendez's career.

Teaming Across Boundaries

Mendez, the houseguests, the Canadians who sheltered them, and the creative artists in Hollywood who made it all believable had little in common. They came from different backgrounds, different organizations, different areas of expertise, and different cultures. Yet they collaborated to execute a remarkable and remarkably innovative operation. This kind of diversity involves boundaries between people from different identity groups.

Education (level and type), along with the socializing processes that occur when we interact with others in our field, contributes to unconscious beliefs that the knowledge shared by one's own group is especially important. The knowledge and skills we learn in a given field of expertise make up the visible curriculum. Most people take the knowledge that lies on their side of a boundary for granted. This can make it hard to communicate with those on the other side. But at its core, teaming is about reaching across or spanning such boundaries. To do this, we must first be keenly aware of what they are and what they do.

Taken-for-granted assumptions are hard to recognize. The first step in doing so is becoming aware that they exist, so you can be on the lookout for them.

Types of Boundaries

Three types of boundaries are particularly important in the context of teaming to innovate: physical distance (location, time zone, and so on), status (perceived social value, hierarchical level, profession, and so on), and knowledge (experience, education, and so on).

Physical Distance

In many companies, work teams in globally dispersed locations—so-called virtual teams—are used to integrate expertise. They're virtual because they work together using communication technologies like email, phone, or Skype. The potential for innovation from such teaming is great; however, the challenges are equally so. Without face-to-face contact, taken-for-granted assumptions can be particularly tricky to recognize and address.

Status

The most common status differences at work are profession-based status and level in the organizational hierarchy. Professional status particularly influences speaking-up behavior. In health care, for example, physicians have more status and power than nurses, who in turn have more status than technicians. Yet members across these professions almost always have to team up to take care of patients. So patients are at risk if people don't learn how to team across status boundaries.

Knowledge

Teaming to innovate is most often about bridging across areas of expertise. In product and process development teams, in particular, bringing together people from different organizational functions for a limited period of intense teaming is increasingly common. In product development, engineering offers insight into design and technology;

manufacturing, into feasible production processes, accurate cost estimates, and pilot and full-scale production; and marketing, into customer receptivity, customer segments, product positioning, and product plans. Combining these diverse skill sets and perspectives is as crucial as it is challenging, because misunderstandings arise due to different meanings embedded in different disciplines, and mistrust often follows.

Organization and occupation are both important sources of knowledge boundaries. Organizational boundaries exist anytime people from different companies—or even sites within a company—have to work together. Occupational boundaries come from the training or education through which experts gain mastery over a specialized body of knowledge. This gives them a particular mindset, a way of knowing. And that mastery becomes taken for granted. The jargon acquired in specialized education and practice constitutes a kind of foreign language for others. This makes working together—across the "thought worlds" of occupational communities—vulnerable to misunderstanding.

Meanwhile, in most fields specialization is intensifying. The rate of new knowledge development requires people to invest considerable time just to stay current. This, of course, makes it even harder to master other disciplines. In technical fields the explosion of new knowledge makes narrow specialization especially likely. Fields spawn new subfields, and they in turn spawn even more specialized subfields.

Innovation requires teaming across knowledge boundaries. Whether developing a new cell phone or discovering a cure for diabetes, it is essential to find novelty and synergy from the unexpected combinations of ideas and techniques that can occur between fields of expertise.

What It Takes to Team

The time pressures we all experience today mean that a highly structured approach, in which managers plan each aspect of a large innovation project is unrealistic. Such planning becomes even less realistic when completed tasks are "thrown over the wall" to other functions or disciplines. Instead, the walls between disciplines have to come down, and simultaneous work on related tasks must be coordinated and negotiated.

Nowadays, it's just not possible for even expert individuals to develop important innovations all by themselves. The chances of individual parts coming together into meaningful, functional wholes without intense communication across boundaries are exceedingly low. How can the boundaries between diverse groups be overcome? Curiosity, psychological safety, and process guidelines are three of the key ingredients.

Mutual Curiosity

Genuine curiosity about what others think, worry about, and aspire to achieve is invaluable for crossing boundaries. By cultivating our own curiosity about what makes others tick, each of us can contribute to creating an environment where it's acceptable to express interest in others' thoughts and feelings. MIT professor Ed Schein, a preeminent researcher on corporate culture, uses the term *temporary cultural island* in his description of a process for sharing crucial professional and personal information in a multicultural work group. (Note that the term *culture* applies to nations, companies, professions, and other identity groups.) The process involves talking about concrete experiences and feelings and is fueled by thoughtful questions on the part of a leader acting as a facilitator. Schein explains that cultural assumptions related to authority and intimacy are crucial issues in culturally diverse teams. When someone in one culture violates an authority rule that is taken for granted in another culture, for example by speaking in an overly familiar manner to a high-status person, someone may experience the behavior as jarring. When we share stories in which these issues are exposed, boundaries begin to dissolve.

Psychological Safety

Boundaries will not be spanned, and innovation cannot flourish in an environment that lacks psychological safety. Psychological safety describes an interpersonal climate where people feel able to express ideas, ask questions, quickly acknowledge mistakes, and raise concerns about the project early and often. They also feel responsible for doing so. It's not that it's easy for them to take these interpersonal risks; rather, they understand it's expected of them. It is part of collaboration. They recognize, too, that teaming up is as interpersonally challenging as it is rewarding. Without these behaviors—which can feel especially risky in hierarchies—successful innovation is unlikely. Table 10.1 depicts leadership actions that help build a climate of psychological safety where innovation can thrive.

Table 10.1   Leadership Behaviors That Build Psychological Safety

Behavior	Description
Acknowledge limits.	When leaders admit that they don't know something, their genuine display of humility encourages other team members to follow suit.
Invite participation.	When people believe their leaders value their input, they're more engaged and responsive.
Use direct language.	Using direct, actionable language instigates the type of straightforward, blunt discussion that enables learning.

In fast-paced, cross-disciplinary, cross-border teaming, it's not easy for people to quickly share their ideas and expertise. Some people worry about what others will think of them. Some fear that they will be less valuable if they give away what they know. Others are reluctant to show off. Even accepting others' ideas can be difficult if it feels like an admission of weakness. Because vital interpersonal exchanges don't always happen spontaneously, leaders must facilitate them. A basic approach to creating psychological safety as a leader is to model the behaviors on which teaming depends, such as asking thoughtful questions or acknowledging your own ignorance about a topic or area of expertise. Leaders who act this way make it safer for everyone else to do it, too.

Process Guidelines

In any complex teaming effort, it is important to establish process guidelines that everyone agrees to follow. A strategy for boundary management is essential. Guidelines are needed for specifying points at which separate teaming activities must come together to coordinate resources and decisions.

When Conflict Heats Up

Even when psychological safety, curiosity, and process guidelines are in place, the very nature of teaming is such that conflict will occur. In fact, conflict is desirable. Without conflict—the competing ideas from which new possibilities sometimes spring—innovation is less likely. But however appealing the idea of creative conflict is in theory, in practice managing conflict effectively is hard to do.

The trouble is, when we encounter differences of opinion, especially those based on values or beliefs we hold deeply, it can trigger strong emotions. Emotions can hijack reason, temporarily of course, making it hard to sift through the differences and find the important questions, ideas, and new possibilities that may be lurking. It takes skill to cool one's own and others' emotions so as to put conflict to good use.

What set of skills is necessary to transform hot tensions into creativity and innovation? It starts with understanding the difference between hot and cool cognition.

Hot and Cool Cognition

Research by cognitive psychologists Janet Metcalfe and Walter Mischel showed that we each have two distinct cognitive systems through which we process events, which they called *hot* and *cool*. The hot system, when engaged, triggers people to respond emotionally and quickly. In this case they are often said to speak or act in the heat of the moment. The cool system, by contrast, is deliberate and careful. When using our cool system, we can slow down and gather our thoughts. The cool system is the basis for self-regulation and self-control. It is desperately needed to team effectively in the face of conflict. Think about the last time you found yourself debating an important issue at work, especially one you really cared about. Many such conversations go back and forth, with people repeating the same points over and over again. Conflicts heat up when people hold different values or belief systems, or have different interests and incentives. This can make it hard to process the conflict productively, and hard to find the seeds of something new and innovative.

Such conflicts often quickly reach an impasse, and the discussion gets personal. It's hard for people not to see each other's viewpoint as wrongheaded, and deliberately so. Each sees the other as stubborn or, worse, manipulative. They fall victim to what's called the *fundamental attribution error*, as we discussed in week 2. And whether blaming each other's motives, character, or abilities, people in the midst of a tough conflict usually silently blame someone else for the lack of progress on the issues. Although very human, this spontaneous reasoning severely hampers innovation.

Three Practices That Cool Hot Conflict

The key question is this: how can people effectively use different perspectives to produce innovation rather than unproductive conflict? The answer lies in understanding how to cool hot topics in fast-paced conversations at work. I recommend three practices to cool down conflict.

Manage Self

This practice involves recognizing one's emotions for what they are: spontaneous personal reactions to a situation. Emotions let us know that we care about the discussion at hand, and we need to slow ourselves down to pay very close attention to what's happening. Managing self means learning how to quickly reflect—to turn our curiosity inward for a brief period and ask ourselves why we're feeling anxious, or frustrated, or angry. It's critical to remind oneself in these situations of two essential facts. First is the very real likelihood that you are missing part of the picture (the part that others see!). Second is that you too are contributing to the problem—in the same way you're convinced the other person is doing so.

Manage Conversations

This practice starts with realizing that conversations don't manage themselves. It takes a bit of guidance for a conversation that has crossed knowledge boundaries and run into conflicting perspectives to go well and produce good results. To facilitate good communication in the face of heated conflict, it's necessary to slow the conversation down so as to combine thoughtful statements with thoughtful questions. This enables people to understand the true basis of a disagreement and to identify the rationale behind different positions. Doing this well also means inviting quiet voices into the discussion to bring new perspectives and new facts to light.

Manage Relationships

While the first two practices are skills that are needed in the heat of a disagreement, the third is the ongoing practice of building strong relationships that can withstand the temporary assault of disagreement. Managers who take the time to get to know each other as people and to understand the other's goals and concerns are less likely to attribute selfish motives to each other and more likely to be curious about others' concerns. Managing relationships is about building trust grounded in experience. Investing time in getting to know colleagues—new and old—helps lay the foundation for productive conflict, despite the emotions that will surely surface along the way.

It's not possible to manage conflict by simply avoiding emotions. Our emotions are spontaneous and natural. To suggest we avoid them in difficult conversations is a fool's errand. Instead, we have to learn how to be thoughtful and open about them. We have to be willing to dig a little more deeply into what they are telling us. This is essential because innovation almost always involves the effective use of differences. Learning how to talk about what makes us tick and what lies underneath our opinions helps to build the genuine, resilient relationships that are crucial to effective teaming.

Embracing the Risks of Teaming

Innovation involves people. And people, as we all know, are complicated creatures. Because innovation requires problem-solving on so many levels, from practical skills to expertise and creativity, teaming to innovate often involves a great deal of diversity. In fact, the greater the diversity among team members—in backgrounds, skills, and expertise—the greater the likelihood of success, but also the greater the likelihood of misunderstandings and problematic conflict. The teaming practices you learned this week can help innovation teams overcome these very real challenges to success.

Teaming to Innovate

Innovation is usually a team sport, but the composition of the team and how they work together matters a great deal. In this activity, you'll examine the need for the right team for innovation.

Activity
Reflect on the following questions:

Think back to the most successful team you've ever been a part of. What was the degree of diverse expertise or perspectives on the team? Could some members of the team be described as strange bedfellows? If so, why do you think the team worked so well?

_____

_____

_____

Of the three boundaries discussed this week that teaming can cross (physical distance, status, and knowledge), which do you think is the toughest to overcome? What strategies have you used in the past to get around this boundary?

_____

_____

_____

How important is it to you to feel camaraderie with your team? Do you believe it's possible to be a part of an effective team if there is no camaraderie? Why or why not?

_____

_____

_____

Of the three skills for cooling conflict discussed this week (managing self, conversation, and relationships), is there one that you often struggle with? What strategies could you use to gain mastery over this skill?

_____

_____

_____

Week 11

Failing to Succeed

Benchmark goal: Fail well: See how failure sets the stage for success.

Every child learns at some point that failure is bad, and dodging blame is a winning strategy. By the time we're working adults, avoiding association with failure is all but second nature. This self-protective reflex may keep our reputation intact (or at least most people seem to think it does), but it harms the companies we work for. Why? It is nearly impossible to learn from failures if people don't admit and analyze them. In any industry where innovation is crucial for survival, an ability to learn from failure is an essential skill.

Learning from failure thus begins with unlearning. This is because childish notions of success are intimately twined with self-esteem, status, and the need for approval. As adults we understand that knowledge is in constant flux, technology insists on changing fast, and confronting new and unfamiliar situations is simply part of working in the twenty-first century. Expecting failure-free performance is illogical in this dynamic context. Moreover, if we want to innovate, we must unlearn spontaneous responses about failure. We must reprogram. Unlearning the idea that failure is bad starts with a deeper understanding of failure.

Unpacking Failure

Over the last 20 years of research and consulting within organizations in a variety of industries, I've seen managers really struggle to embrace the reality that failure is an essential prerequisite to innovation. In fact, the exhortation to fail well sounds to them like a nonsensical oxymoron. This is because they haven't fully recognized that failures come in several different types, not all (in fact, few) of them blameworthy.

I will describe three basic types of failure: basic, complex, and intelligent. I'll also talk about how to design intelligent failures and how to be courageous. Avoiding basic failures is both important and feasible. Complex failures can be hard to predict, but with vigilance they too can be largely avoided. By contrast, intelligent failures are in fact positive events. They're part of an essential strategy for creating new knowledge, developing ideas, and producing innovation. Failing well means engaging in intelligent failures. It also means learning quickly when complex failures occur, or nearly occur, so as to avoid any future recurrence. A primary aspect of failing well is avoiding the "blame game" so that you can use failure to promote innovation.

Many leaders worry that in the absence of blame there's no accountability, and without accountability employees won't work hard. The truth is, a culture that makes it safe to be honest, safe to report failure, and safe to admit mistakes is a culture in which a responsible adult can thrive and do their best work. Why? Because most people want to feel proud of the work they do, to be part of something larger than themselves, and to make a difference in the lives of colleagues and customers. Given the right conditions, they will.

Failure's Causes

Let's start with the obvious cause. Deliberate violation, in which a person chooses to violate a prescribed procedure or rule, clearly anchors the blameworthy end of the spectrum. Inattention, in which someone inadvertently deviates from what's required because they lost focus or got distracted—well, that's a little less clear. Inattention could be due to texting when you should be looking at the road. That's blameworthy. Or it could occur when a worker is put in the problematic situation of working a double shift, and fatigue has made perfect attentiveness impossible. There's blame involved here, but it belongs to the manager who put the worker in that situation, not to the worker. Next on my spectrum is lack of competence. This describes a situation in which an individual doesn't have or hasn't been taught the necessary skills to do the job (hmmm, whose fault is that?).

Inadequate process describes a situation in which an individual, or a group, faces a faulty or incomplete set of guidelines. This often occurs when a process is new, and the kinks haven't been worked out yet. Task challenge describes situations in which the task at hand is simply too difficult to be successfully executed every time. For a simple illustration, consider the elite figure skater able to perform the extraordinary feat of a quadruple Lutz to embellish a winning Olympic routine. Given that no skater pulled off this extremely difficult move in a competition until 2011, it's clear that the quadruple Lutz is too challenging to support a realistic expectation that any skater can do it perfectly every time. When a failure to execute an exceedingly challenging task occurs, it would be just plain wrong to call that blameworthy.

Next, some situations are exceedingly complex. When Hurricane Sandy hit New York City in fall 2012, responding successfully meant bringing an enormous number of different people and actions to bear on a fast-moving problem with many affected people, buildings, and organizations. Even though good protocols were in place for hurricane response, complexity means that it was unlikely that everything would work perfectly—that is, that no failures (small or large) would occur along the way. New York's emergency response system performed admirably, but this didn't mean that nothing went wrong and no one got hurt.

Relatedly, uncertainty means we don't have complete knowledge about future events. Given what they know at the time, people will take reasonable actions that nonetheless may produce undesirable results (failures). Note that it would be unreasonable to blame anyone for such failures; the appropriate reaction would be something like, "We did the best we could with the knowledge we had."

Finally, some failures happen as a result of experimentation. Consider two kinds of experiments. First, hypothesis-testing experiments test a specific prediction. They might be focused on whether a new packaging design will appeal to customers, for example. Sometimes our hypotheses are right. Sometimes they are wrong (failure again!). Either way, we've learned something. It's better to find out that customers don't like the packaging before we roll it out at full scale. Exploratory experiments, in contrast to experiments driven by a focused hypothesis, are conducted to investigate a possibility, without a strong sense of what we expect to happen. They expand our knowledge of some area through exploratory action.

Considering the range of causes along this spectrum, it should be clear that deliberate violation is the only action for which a person obviously deserves to be blamed. After that, from inattention all the way through to exploratory experiments, it would be harder to come to that conclusion. This would require us to ignore the effects of fatigue, poor training, poor management, or novelty (see Table 11.1). In fact, any failure resulting from honest effort or thoughtful experimentation is grist for the innovation mill and thus should instead be considered praiseworthy.

Table 11.1   A Spectrum of Potential Causes of Organizational Failures

Potential Cause of Failure	Description	Is Blame Appropriate?
Deliberate violation	An individual chooses to violate a prescribed process or practice.	Yes
Inattention	An individual inadvertently deviates from a prescribed process or practice.	Maybe
Lack of ability	An individual doesn't have the skills, conditions, or training to execute a job.	Unlikely
Inadequate process	An individual adheres to a prescribed process, but the process is faulty or incomplete.	Unlikely
Task challenge	An individual faces a task that is too difficult to be executed reliably every time.	Doubtful
Complexity	A process composed of many elements breaks down when novel interactions take place.	Rarely
Uncertainty	Lacking sufficient knowledge of future events, people take reasonable actions that nonetheless produce undesired results.	No

(continued)

Failing to Succeed

Table 11.1 *(continued)*

Potential Cause of Failure	Description	Is Blame Appropriate?
Hypothesis-testing experiment	An experiment conducted to test a prediction that a particular design or course of action will produce a particular result fails to confirm the hypothesis.	No
Exploratory experiment	An experiment conducted to expand knowledge and investigate a possibility leads to an undesired result.	No

I've shared this spectrum of causes with executives from a range of industries and asked them to estimate what percentage of the failures in their organization might be caused by blameworthy actions. Usually, they pick a number that is less than 5 percent. Then I ask how often failures in their company are actually treated as blameworthy. After a pause (or an uncomfortable laugh), they come up with a much higher number, say 70–90 percent. The discrepancy (between less than 5 and 90) is a far greater problem than most managers realize. If thoughtful managers understand that failures do happen, and that it's rare when an individual can rightly be blamed, then they'll also see that to engage in blaming is more than just illogical. It's counterproductive.

Why? Because valuable failures go unreported. Failure's lessons are lost. The real cost of blaming people for bad outcomes—when the real causes are uncertainty or complexity, for example—is that innovation is hampered. To understand this better, take a look at three kinds of failure.

Mapping the Failure Landscape

Although an infinite number of things can go wrong in organizations, they fall into three broad categories of failure: basic, complexity-related, and intelligent. The causes discussed in this chapter correspond roughly, and in sets of three, to these three failure types. In this 90-Day Plan, we are particularly interested in intelligent failures at the frontier (the frontier being where innovation occurs). But intelligent failures are best understood by contrasting them to the other types.

Basic Failures

Most failures in this category can indeed be considered "bad" in the sense that they were highly basic. They may involve unwarranted deviation from a well-defined process in a routine operation. In fact, they are particularly relevant in the context of routine operations, that is, when knowledge for how to do things "right" is available. Although rarely deliberate, such deviations are almost always avoidable. With proper training and support, steps in a routine process can and should be followed consistently. Failure to do so is usually due to one of the first three of the nine reasons for failure in the spectrum (violation, inattention, or lack of ability). When that happens, the causes can be readily identified and solutions developed.

In innovation projects, experiments that have been run before and failed but are inadvertently run again qualify as basic failures. Optimal practice for innovation is not to avoid failure, but it does avoid producing the same failure twice.

Complex Failures

Many organizational failures are the result of system complexity and are not completely preventable. When a particular combination of needs, people, and problems has never occurred before—such as triaging patients in a hospital emergency room, troubleshooting in a major IT installation, or running a fast-growing start-up—at least some small failures must be expected. To assume otherwise would be illogical. System failure also is a perpetual risk in complex organizations like aircraft carriers, nuclear power plants, and air traffic control.

While serious failures may be averted by following risk management best practices, including a thorough analysis of all near-miss events (as I discuss in week 12), small process failures will inevitably occur. To consider them "bad" is a misunderstanding of how complex systems work. It is also counterproductive. It blocks the rapid identification and correction of small failures that is crucial to avoiding consequential failures. The majority of failures experienced by hospitalized patients—massive heparin overdoses that harmed babies in two separate hospitals a few years ago, for instance—occur as a result of a series of small process failures that unfortunately lined up in just the wrong way to allow patients to be harmed. Best practice means catching and correcting these small failures before this happens, because, again, small failures will occur in complex, customized work. Major failures, however, can be prevented through vigilance, good communication, and proactive learning. (For all of these behaviors, of course, psychological safety is critical.)

Intelligent Failures

The most important insight for managers seeking to promote innovation is that failures in this category aren't in fact "bad" at all. Indeed, intelligent failures can rightly be considered "good." They provide valuable new knowledge that can help a team to come up with innovative products and help a company to grow. Intelligent failures occur when experimentation is necessary—when answers are not knowable in advance (because we've never been in this exact situation before and probably never will again). Discovering and testing new drugs, creating a radically new business, developing a new biofuel, creating a prototype for an energy-efficient vehicle, and testing customer reactions in a new market are examples of undertakings where this is the case. These are tasks that demand intelligent failure. And the faster the failures happen, the better.

This kind of experimentation is often referred to as *trial and error*, but that is a misnomer. *Error* implies that you could have done it right the first time and that not doing so constitutes a mistake. But a trial is needed precisely when results are not knowable in advance. For this reason, I call the experimentation process *trial and failure*. (We lack a word that means "unpreventable novel failures," which itself is telling.)

Failing Well—At the Right Scale

When you're exploring the frontier, the right kind of experimentation is one that produces good failures quickly and intelligently, which is why Professor Sim Sitkin at Duke calls them intelligent failures, despite the apparent oxymoron. Managers who work with failures in this fashion are more likely to get the most out of them—and also to avoid the unintelligent failure of conducting experiments on a scale that is larger than necessary.

As an example, in the late 1990s a major telecommunications company I'll refer to as Telco set out to innovate. To be positioned at what was then the forefront of new and some-what unproven technology, Telco decided to launch digital subscriber line technology, or DSL, to provide its customers with high-speed internet service. In its well-intentioned desire to innovate, however, Telco made the mistake of experimenting at too large a scale.

Despite the very real operational risks of the unproven new technology, Telco launched DSL throughout its entire market, all at once, and before the company was really able to deliver it reliably. The outcome, unfortunately, was a dismal failure. Customer satisfaction, usually in the high 80s, dove down to the teens. As many as 500 customers a day were waiting to hear back about some aspect of service. Twenty percent of complaints were taking 30 or more days to resolve. Customers were frustrated and angry, and employee morale suffered as well.

Of course, Telco's mistake did not lie in trying to innovate, or even in experiencing failure as part of the innovation process. The mistake was that it launched an experiment—an uncertain new service operation—at such a large and painful scale. By rolling DSL out to the entire market, rather than launching a small pilot that could help it see what worked (and what didn't), Telco lost the chance to make rapid changes as a result of thoughtful experimentation. The company converted what could have been an intelligent failure into a preventable (not-so-intelligent) failure. At that point in time, the process knowledge for how to deliver the new service reliably across diverse customer situations was simply underdeveloped. Not considering this mismatch, Telco was in a position of managing an initiative that should have been treated as a complex new operation, not as a routine operation.

By contrast, IDEO, the global product design consultancy, set out to launch a new kind of innovation strategy service. Traditionally, IDEO helped clients design new products within their existing product lines. The new service would assist clients in identifying new strategic product line opportunities. Knowing it had not worked out all the details for delivering the new services effectively, IDEO started with a small project with a low-tech manufacturing client so as to learn from an early small experiment. Although the project failed—the client did not change its product strategy—IDEO learned from it. The company then figured out what it had to do differently, including developing new processes for understanding clients' businesses and hiring staff with MBAs who had experience diagnosing and developing business strategy. Today, strategic services account for more than a third of IDEO's revenues.

We can sing the praises of intelligent failure as much as we want. But that inner child, the one who wants to be right and is terrified of being wrong, doesn't just go gently into that good night. That's where leadership comes in.

Leading Failure

As we've seen, failing well means tolerating unavoidable process failures in complex systems and celebrating intelligent failures at the frontier of knowledge. Rather than promoting mediocrity, such tolerance is essential for any team or organization seeking the new knowledge that failure in complex and novel settings provides.

Strategically producing failures takes this one step further. Researchers in basic science know that once in a great while an experiment yields a spectacular success. However, more often (far more often!) experiments result in failure. Scientists can't succeed unless they learn to recognize failure as a step on the path to success. Remember from week 8 the chief scientific officer at pharmaceutical giant Eli Lilly who threw failure parties to celebrate clinical trials or scientific programs that were intelligent but that nonetheless failed? This odd ritual makes scientists more willing to take intelligent risks, but it also encourages them to speak up sooner rather than later about a failing course of action. Failing is neither blameworthy nor shameful, but part of a valiant effort to generate new knowledge.

Most managers in business, however, feel a great deal of pressure to make sure that their product or service is perfect when it goes out into the world. This pressure affects the pilot projects that are designed to test the new idea. Managers are so eager to succeed (understandably!) that they often design pilots that incorporate optimal conditions rather than representative ones. The result? Fragile successes. A pilot is meant to generate knowledge about what won't work, not simply affirm the genius behind an innovation. Pilots must be designed to fail.

To understand why, consider the Telco failure again. Before the full-scale urban launch, managers had run a small pilot in a suburb that housed well-educated, tech-savvy customers. The pilot was considered a soaring success. Unfortunately, pilot conditions were anything but representative of the large and diverse urban market in which the full-scale launch would take place. To make matters worse, the pilot was staffed by particularly expert and friendly service reps who were well versed in the new technology and could make it work for any customer's home computer setup. This small pilot was not so much a hypothesis-testing experiment as a demonstration project. It was designed to succeed—rather than to fail intelligently so that the subsequent full-scale launch could be a success.

What should Telco have done? First, the technology should have been tested in a small and unsophisticated market (old computers, fewer tech-savvy customers), with normal staffing levels to support it. The pilot should have been designed to uncover every little thing that could possibly go wrong—before announcing the new service to all customers. Managers would have been poised to reward intelligent failures and to help teams learn from them quickly to improve the product as well as the service that accompanied it. To generalize this lesson, I list a few questions that should be answered in the affirmative when designing the right kind of pilot projects—the kind that fail intelligently.

As these questions demonstrate, managers hoping to successfully launch an innovative or novel product should not try to produce success the first time around. Instead, they should attempt to design and execute the most informative trial-and-failure process possible. This strategy for learning from pilot-size failures is a way to ensure that full-scale, online services will succeed.

Managers of successful pilots must be able to answer yes to the following questions:

- Is the pilot program being tested under typical circumstances instead of optimal conditions?

- Are the employees, customers, and resources representative of the firm's real operating environment?

- Is the goal of the pilot to learn as much as possible rather than demonstrate to senior managers the value of the new system?

- Is the goal of learning as much as possible understood by everyone involved, including employees and managers?

- Is it clear that compensation and performance ratings are not based on a successful outcome of the pilot?

- Were explicit changes made as a result of the pilot program?

Courage and Fear

Like the cowardly lion in *The Wizard of Oz*, we have to learn that fear and courage exist side by side. The lion didn't understand at first that courage does not mean an absence of fear but a willingness to act in spite of fear.

Confronting failure means confronting our imperfection. This takes courage because, of course, it is unpleasant. But acknowledging our limits with good nature and a sense of humor enables us to get on with things to be creative and innovative. Environments that discourage the reporting of problems, mistakes, and failures block this forward movement, this learning. Managers who ask employees to be brave and to speak up must not later express disapproval or even anger. Rather, gratitude is called for when an employee reveals the complex systems at work behind organizational failures. Then the real innovation can begin.

Managers are often concerned, as I've mentioned, that embracing failure will create a messy, anarchic, anything-goes environment in which nothing ever gets done. But this simply isn't the case. One does not follow from the other. The fact is, failure is inevitable, especially in today's complex knowledge economy. Learning from failure, even moving in that direction, will give any organization a competitive edge.

Tom Kelley (general manager of IDEO) and David Kelley (founder and chairman) have written about the importance of what they call *creative confidence*: "the natural ability to come up with new ideas and the courage to try them out." They put this into action in their company by giving employees "strategies to get past four fears that hold most of us back: fear of the messy unknown, fear of being judged, fear of the first step, and fear of losing control."[1]

No matter what kind of failure occurs, avoid playing the blame game—the pull to name culprits rather than causes. This game is deeply counterproductive. Get comfortable with the mindset that identifies failure as an inevitable, valuable part of the innovation journey.

Of course, failure is not worth much if we don't learn from it (and learn fast!). Let's look at what it takes to do that well.

Failing the Right Way

Failure can be a good thing, but only under the right conditions. In this activity, you'll take a look at productive failures.

Activity

Reflect on the following questions:

Three types of failure are discussed this week: basic, complexity-related, and intelligent. As you think of your own career, think of a time that you experienced each of these types of failures: which was the hardest? What "good" failures have you experienced? What did they enable you to do, subsequently?

_____

_____

_____

Of the three boundaries to teaming discussed in this week (physical distance, status, and knowledge), which do you think is the toughest to overcome? What strategies have you used in the past to get around this boundary?

_____

_____

_____

What does "failing at the right scale" mean to you?

_____

_____

_____

Do you agree that learning rather than demonstrating is the better goal for a pilot program? Why or why not?

_____

_____

_____

Learning from Failure

Benchmark goal: Learn fast: Make the most of your failure.

In companies, learning fast is a team sport. Although individual employees learn in a casual way all the time (having new insights, improving their skills), this type of learning doesn't automatically help the company to perform better. Individual participation in formal training programs doesn't either. Here, we look at what it takes for organizations to systematically learn from the vast array of experiences they have—especially from failure.

Everyone agrees that people and organizations should learn from failure. And yet organizations that systematically and effectively learn from failure are very rare. This is because learning fast requires discipline. It is systematic and effortful. I explicate four steps of the learning process that underlies innovation. Of course, there are barriers to learning inherent in each of these steps, and we'll take a look at how some companies overcome them. Finally, I give some tips for leading learning in the context of innovation.

Deliberate learning from experience starts with the right managerial mindset. I call it *organizing to learn*. It's a way of thinking and acting that is driven by the recognition that the world keeps changing, and that today's answers are almost certainly not tomorrow's. It means not having too much (unwarranted) faith in our first round of ideas. For instance, recall the Telco DSL launch described in week 11. Senior management's (unsubstantiated) faith in the company's ability to deliver led to a premature full-scale rollout in a large and diverse urban market.

Learning as You Go

The Telco failure happened because the company went all out with an innovation without accurately assessing its own current operational capabilities. Imagine that instead of a full-scale, widely advertised rollout, Telco had engaged a few pioneering customers who tolerated some imperfections in the brand-new service and also gave the company feedback to help it improve the service quickly. As coinvestigators, these pioneers might have even enjoyed helping the company find the weak spots. Together, company and customer would learn as they went. Before long, the problems would be solved and the kinks worked out in an inevitable march toward a reliable, easy-to-use innovation, which future customers would take for granted. As one might roll out a carpet, a rollout implies that something is ready to go, just needing a bit of momentum to propel it forward. Cycling out, by contrast, is a journey punctuated with deliberate and thoughtful iteration and learning.

Any company trying to innovate must figure out a way to learn as quickly as possible from early experiences (preferably at a small scale) in the life of the project. There are no shortcuts. To provide a compelling new product or service that works and appeals to a wide range of customers, you have to be willing to start with one that doesn't work well. It means taking seriously the adage of nineteenth-century British philosopher G. K. Chesterton: "If something's worth doing, it's worth doing badly." Of course, just doing something badly (before you figure out how to do it well) isn't enough. To learn fast from experience, managers have to deliberately frame the early-stage experiences as experiments. Experiments generate data—and data must be learned from.

On the innovation journey, each step is an experiment, and each experiment must be different from the one before. Its design must incorporate the knowledge gained in the prior cycle. In this way, an innovation cycles out, bumpily, improving as it expands. For example, Netflix introduced its Watch Instantly offering in successive waves of 250,000 customers, taking six months to cycle out its instant downloading technology; during this time, the company constantly checked in with customers via follow-up emails that inquired about the quality of specific movies watched. It also set up and actively monitored a Netflix blog to explain operations, step-by-step, and to respond to frequent customer posts regarding problems, requests, and suggestions. The service was essentially free for several years, until the problems were worked out. Once it really worked smoothly, Netflix asked customers to pay. This is the kind of practice that companies use to learn fast. Above all, innovation requires companies to fully use employee and customer experiences for learning.

How to Learn Fast

Learning in general, and especially for innovation, involves four essential steps: diagnosing the situation, challenge, or problem (including assessing what is currently known about it); designing initial actions; taking action (viewed as experimenting); and reflecting to gain the lessons from the experiment.

Diagnosis

Diagnosis involves sizing up the situation and the challenges that might lie ahead. It's about identifying the opportunities for innovation—the subtle customer desires or pain points that haven't yet been addressed by viable products or services. Diagnosis may range from extended study of customer behaviors to behind-the-scenes analysis of large data sets to a quick exchange of ideas between colleagues about opportunities.

At Intuit, the financial software company, engineers directly observe customers as they interact with the software so as to evaluate how easy or difficult it is for them to use the features built into the product. This enables engineers to observe unmet user needs firsthand, needs that customers themselves lack either the experience or the vocabulary to voice. Another part of diagnosis for innovation is assessing what's feasible, given the current state of technology or the costs of inputs. Opportunities may be wide, but they are not infinite.

Design

The next step is to identify possibilities for action. Design is done when a team has a preliminary commitment to action—whether through a formal decision or plan, or by a gradual shift into agreement to try something out. The purpose of design in innovation is to guide action. That may sound oversimple, but design fosters learning by making action more deliberate and conscious.

At Motorola, one of the most successful innovations in the company's history was the RAZR phone, introduced back in 2004. That innovation was the result of a motivated team's efforts to brainstorm shapes and features for the phone and then to quickly try out mockups made of clay before getting too far down the path with real materials. As in this example, the design step in any innovation journey is often just a starting point. It may lead to only a single step forward, one that we expect to revise as soon as we learn more. Thus, in an innovation project, a focus group might be used to react to an experimental new service or product idea before we figure out all of the details of execution.

Action or Experimentation

The shift from talking to doing, from considering to trying, also happens in teams. A key to effective action in execution-as-learning is making sure to track what actually happens as well as tracking the results of the action. Traditional management controls emphasize outcome data, which capture results. Execution-as-learning pays just as much attention to process data, which describe how work unfolds.

Rapid, unconstrained action is at the heart of innovation. It's called *experimentation*. Scientists, of course, routinely experiment, hoping to be first to make an important discovery in the process. Experiments range from those for which possible outcomes are all but unknown in advance to those in which strong hypotheses are being tested. In basic research, a scientist who has a 70 percent failure rate in the experiments they run might be in the process of earning a Nobel Prize. The RAZR team tried out several configurations before hitting on its revolutionary slimming design, by putting the battery next to the circuit board (prior phones had them stacked) to reduce thickness. Teams at IDEO routinely build quick prototypes to see what new products might look like in three dimensions. The point is simply to try things and see what happens. It's easy to stay in the conceptual plane—to talk about ideas and possibilities forever. A key to successful innovation is making frequent, small forays into action.

Reflection

After taking action, it's critical to take some time to understand what happened: what worked and what didn't. Reflection is about digging into failures, intelligent or otherwise. It's an analytic task.

Innovation teams have to learn fast from the trials and failures they produce so that they can conduct new trials as soon as possible. Reflecting on failure is rarely fun, but it's essential to figuring out the true causes of a failure in order to determine what gets tried next. Don't shortchange reflection in the desire to move quickly to the next experiment, because high-quality reflection can help avoid predictable failures in subsequent actions. Ed Catmull, founder and president of Pixar, lamented that Pixar employees would just as soon avoid post-project reflection altogether, preferring to relish the success of a film than to stop and identify what could have gone better. To get more out of this critical step, he instituted the following: participants are asked to list five things they would do again, and then to discuss five things they wouldn't do. According to Catmull, this positive-negative balance created a safe environment conducive to discussing every aspect of a project thoughtfully.

It's not easy for any company facing cost constraints (and who isn't!) to stop and reflect. Disciplined evaluation takes productive resources offline, and conventional management wisdom views this as lost productivity. Nonetheless, the only way to achieve and sustain excellence is for leaders to insist that their organizations invest resources in the reflection that makes innovation possible.

Overcoming Barriers to Learning

Learning from failure is a hallmark of innovative companies. But it requires an unusual mindset and systematic effort, and companies that do it well are rare. Why? Because there are barriers to innovation at each step of the learning process.

Barriers to Diagnosis

Diagnosis sets the stage for learning from the inevitable failures in any innovation process. This is where opportunities are assessed and aspirational goals are revisited (remember "aim high"). Because most people experience strong negative feelings about failure, these kinds of conversations must be managed thoughtfully.

This story illustrates a pervasive and fundamental problem. Although many methods of surfacing current and pending failures exist, they are grossly underused in today's organizations. For instance, total quality management and soliciting feedback from customers are well-known techniques for bringing failures to light. But too many messengers—even the most senior executives—are reluctant to convey bad news to bosses and colleagues.

It's just not possible to diagnose or predict failure when people don't feel it is safe to express their full thoughts and feelings about the various issues on the table. Leaders have to go out of their way to avoid "shooting the messenger," and to instead encourage people to speak up. Mulally's applause is a great example of how to do that. People must feel able to speak up about both clear and ambiguous signals that something might be amiss. This is essential to innovation! Without evidence that the present is deficient in some way, the motivation to innovate is lacking.

Barriers to Design

For the purposes of organizational learning, the design step is a thoughtful pause that guides subsequent action. The most important barrier to design is a lack of psychological safety. When people are overly worried about what others will think of them, they become reluctant to raise potentially crazy ideas. But innovation benefits from crazy ideas. Sometimes it's the crazy idea—despite being impractical or useless in its own right—that triggers someone else to have a truly innovative and useable idea. It's important in innovation to make sure people feel uninhibited to dream and imagine all sorts of possibilities.

This points to a second barrier. Beyond feeling safe to speak up, people also have to reengage their imaginations, which can sometimes atrophy in corporate hierarchies. A lack of imagination is another important barrier to coming up with designs for action that are new enough—enough of a departure from the status quo—to generate worthwhile experiments. An important leadership task, therefore, is to provoke and nurture imagination, to help people think as broadly as possible about options. Thinking is free, whereas action can be expensive. So the design step should be used to conduct thought experiments through which obviously wrongheaded approaches can be skipped going forward.

Barriers to Action and Experimentation

A lack of psychological safety is also a barrier to the third step in the learning process: deliberate experimentation. If people don't feel safe, they will conduct only very low-risk experiments, where successful outcomes are relatively easy to predict. (This is why managers sometimes conduct pilots that don't yield much information, as described in week 11 in the examination of what it takes to "fail well.") But innovative organizations are willing to conduct (and learn quickly from) experiments that fail.

Consider the example of IDEO, the design firm that promotes internal experimentation through slogans such as "Fail often in order to succeed sooner" and "Enlightened trial-and-error succeeds over the planning of the lone genius." These statements are accompanied by frequent small experiments and much good humor over the associated failures.

In many companies, incentives (formal and informal) are inconsistent with stated values about learning from failure. This makes true experimentation difficult and rare. This obvious barrier to experimentation must be mitigated—by aligning incentives with what it takes to innovate. Those who experiment should be celebrated, and companies must publicize both failures and successes internally, so that all employees can see that the idea of learning from failure is more than just "talk."

A final barrier to effective experimentation is the reluctance people have to call an experiment a failure, even after the data are clearly pointing in that direction. It's important to teach people when to declare defeat in an experimental course of action. The human tendency to hope for the best and avoid failure at all costs gets in the way, and organizational hierarchies exacerbate the problem. As a result, failing research and development (R&D) projects are often kept going much longer than is analytically rational or economically prudent. We throw good money after bad, praying that we'll pull a rabbit out of a hat. Intuition and experience may tell engineers or scientists that a project has fatal flaws, but the formal decision to call it a failure may be delayed for months.

Barriers to Reflection

Organizations cannot learn from failure, and other experiences, without thoughtful analysis and discussion. Again, a lack of psychological safety can be a major barrier to doing this well. Formal processes or forums for discussing, analyzing, and applying the lessons of failure involve direct language and straightforward confrontation of sometimes unwelcome facts. People rarely do this well unless they feel psychologically safe enough to leave their ego at the door and fully engage with the substance of the discussion.

A second major barrier (as we've seen) is blame. After experiencing failure, people typically blame other people or forces beyond their control (like traffic and weather). We tend to downplay our own responsibility and blame external or situational factors when we fail, only to do the reverse when assessing the failures of others—a psychological trap we discussed in week 2 known as *fundamental attribution error.* Leaders have to help groups avoid the blame game and keep attention focused on what can be learned from the prior action or experiment and what that means for the next one. Expert outside (or internal) facilitators can keep a reflection process productive and bring new perspectives and insights that deepen the analysis.

Effective analysis of failure requires both time and space, along with skill in managing the conflicting perspectives that may emerge. Some organizations, like the military, set aside time for after-action reviews; hospitals use morbidity and mortality conferences to discuss significant mistakes or unexpected patient deaths as a forum for identifying, discussing, and learning from failures.

A third barrier is lack of technical or analytic skill. To learn from failed or successful experiments, people need to know how to use basic scientific tools, including the appropriate use of statistical analyses or qualitative data analysis. Relying exclusively on common sense, gut feel, or intuition can lead to flawed conclusions. Even without meaning to, we all favor evidence that supports our existing beliefs over alternative explanations. This is known as *confirmation bias.*

The final barrier is emotional. As previously noted, examining any failure is likely to be emotionally unpleasant. Left to our own devices, most of us will speed through or avoid failure analysis altogether. Reflection takes skill and patience. Yet many managers admire and are rewarded for decisiveness, efficiency, and action—not thoughtful reflection. It takes leadership to push forward against this cultural tide, ensuring that lessons are learned. In the long run, this saves time and promotes the innovation that is so necessary for tomorrow's success.

The goal in reflection is to go beyond first-order reasons (procedures weren't followed) to find second- and third-order explanations for a failure. One way to do this is to use interdisciplinary teams with diverse skills and perspectives. Complex failures in particular are the result of multiple events that occurred in different departments or disciplines or at different levels of the organization. Understanding what happened and how to prevent it from happening again requires detailed, team-based discussion and analysis. Although this takes patience and skill, the benefits for innovation are well worth the investment of managerial effort.

Leading Learning to Innovate

Overcoming the barriers to learning in the pursuit of innovation requires openness, transparency, and, yes, psychological safety. Leaders who wish to promote innovation must work to create and reinforce a culture that counteracts the blame game and makes people feel comfortable with and responsible for surfacing failures and learning from them. The leader's role is to insist on a clear understanding of what happened—not to ask "Who did it?"—when things go wrong.

Framing for Learning

Leaders should also send the right message about the nature of the work, such as reminding people in R&D, "We're in the discovery business, and the faster we fail, the faster we'll succeed." Many managers don't understand or appreciate this subtle but crucial point. To build a culture that is conducive to innovation, managers must create an environment in which everyone can put aside self-protective defenses and approach the work with curiosity and a desire to learn from failure. We cannot underestimate the psychological and interpersonal barriers to this organizational learning process. Reframing failure from something associated with shame and weakness to something that is linked to risk, uncertainty, and improvement is a critical step in the learning journey.

Repeat (Learning Never Stops)

The secret to organizational learning and innovation is that the learning cycle never stops. Once the purpose (where the team is headed) has been established, the process (how we get there) can nearly always be improved.

Team sports have guidelines that move the game forward. Reflection, sharing insights widely in a psychologically safe environment, creating the next experiment, and learning from failures are all crucial steps that move innovation forward. In weeks 9 and 10, I described how to establish a goal and a process. In this week, I looked at how to continuously improve that process to move closer to the goal. Eventually, learning continuously from failure should become second nature—but for now let's just say that it's far more systematic and structured than it might first appear.

In organizations that innovate, learning must become a habit.

Learning from Your Mistakes

Most people take for granted an execution-oriented frame for getting work done. Reframing the work as a learning process is an essential driver of innovation. In this activity, you will examine the value of a learning mindset in innovation.

Activity

Reflect on the following questions:

_____

_____

_____

How did Netflix's rollout of "Watch Instantly" embody the learn-as-you-go approach? What do you think the results would have been if they had rolled it out to all customers for a cost immediately?

_____

_____

_____

What approach did Ed Catmull, founder of Pixar, take to get employees more comfortable with admitting and discussing failure? Do you think this approach would have worked at companies you've worked for?

_____

_____

_____

Do you agree that lack of psychological safety is a barrier to learning from failures? Why or why not?

_____

_____

_____

Wrap-Up

Performance goal: Innovate with teaming.

Teaming to innovate, as many of the examples in this part illustrate, is fueled by a commitment to create a better world in some small or large way. The size of the contribution depends on the kind of work you do and the kind of organization you work in. But no matter where you work, setting out to innovate is an act of hope.

Questions

1. How can people effectively use different perspectives to produce innovation rather than unproductive conflict?

2. Aiming high by setting a challenging goal is an important part of innovation. It means stretching beyond what seems initially feasible. Have you worked on such a goal in your career? Did it lead to innovation?

Activity

For this activity, get a paper and pen to write answers to these prompts.

Describe a time in your career when curiosity (or a lack of it) was an important factor in a team environment. How did it affect the team's ability to meet their goal?

Have you ever encountered a contentious situation on a team? Do you think using one of the key strategies for cooling conflict (managing self, conversations, and relationships) would have helped?

What barriers to learning have you encountered during your career? How do you think they affected your results?

Notes

Chapter 1

1. P. Senge, *The Fifth Discipline: The Art and Practice of the Learning Organization* (New York: Doubleday/Currency, 1990).

Chapter 2

1. L. Ross, "The Intuitive Psychologist and His Shortcomings," *Advances in Experimental Psychology*, Vol. 10, ed. L. Berkowitz (New York: Academic Press, 1977), p. 405.

Chapter 4

1. D. A. Harrison and K. J. Klein, "What's the Difference? Diversity Constructs as Separation, Variety, or Disparity in Organizations," *Academy of Management Review* 32, no. 4 (2007): 1200.
2. A. Tucker and A. C. Edmondson, *"Cincinnati Children's Hospital Medical Center,"* HBS Case No. *609–109* (Boston: Harvard Business School Publishing, 2009), p. 10.

Chapter 11

1. T. Kelley and D. Kelley, "Reclaim Your Confidence," *Harvard Business Review*, December 2012.

Conclusion

Congratulations! You've leveled up your teamwork skills in only 90 days. What you've learned in these 12 weeks will last you for a lifetime of teamwork. I recommend reviewing the weeks that you find most useful or most challenging to brush up occasionally.

Your 90-Day Plan to Level Up Your Teamwork Skills
Performance Goals
• Get ready to learn, innovate, and compete.   • Team fearlessly with psychological safety.   • Innovate with teaming.
Benchmark Goals
Days 1–30   Get ready to learn, innovate, and compete.   Week 1: Understand how teaming is different than teamwork.   Week 2: Learn the four pillars of teaming and why they work.   Week 3: Lead through teaming.   Week 4: Discover how to team across boundaries.

Days 31–60
Team fearlessly with psychological safety.
Week 5: Grasp the power of psychological safety.
Week 6: Make it safe to team.
Week 7: Frame your team for success.
Week 8: Create a fearless organization.
Days 61–90
Innovate with teaming.
Week 9: Aim high.
Week 10: Team up.
Week 11: Fail well.
Week 12: Learn fast.
Personal Goals and Vision for Success
What do you hope to achieve by leveling up?
How could your life change by reaching these goals?

Final Questions

- What tips or suggestions from your 90-Day Plan do you plan to implement in your day-to-day work life?
- Which goals will be most impactful to your career?
- What weeks were the hardest for you and why?
- How do you plan to stay motivated to boost your teamwork skills?

About the Author

Nearing graduation from Harvard College more than three decades ago, Amy Edmondson took a leap of faith and wrote a letter to a personal hero, seeking advice about employment. To her surprise, Buckminster Fuller wrote back. His letter arrived barely a week later with far more than advice. The legendary inventor, architect, and futurist offered her a job. Spending the next three years as Fuller's "chief engineer," she developed an intense and enduring interest in what leaders and organizations can do to create a better world.

Her book *A Fuller Explanation: The Synergetic Geometry of R. Buckminster Fuller* (Boston: Birkhauser, 1987) clarifies Fuller's mathematical contributions for a nontechnical audience. Edmondson received her PhD in organizational behavior, AM in psychology, and AB in engineering and design, all from Harvard University.

Today, as the Novartis professor of leadership and management at the Harvard Business School, Edmondson studies leaders seeking to make a positive difference in the world through the work they do in organizations of all kinds. The research described in this book captures the central thread that has run through her academic career: creating work environments where people can team up and do their best work.

Amy joined the Harvard Business School faculty in 1996 and has taught courses in leadership, organizational learning, and operations management in the MBA and Executive Education programs. Her writings on organizational learning and leadership have been published in more than 60 articles in academic and management journals, and she has consulted widely on these topics for organizations around the world. In 2003, the Academy of Management's Organizational Behavior division selected Edmondson for the Cummings Award for outstanding achievement, and in 2000, it selected her article "Psychological Safety and Learning Behavior in Work Teams" for its annual award for the best published paper in the field. Her article with Anita Tucker, "Why Hospitals Don't Learn from Failures: Organizational and Psychological Dynamics That Inhibit System Change," received the 2004 Accenture Award for significant contribution to management practice.

Before her academic career, she was director of research at Pecos River Learning Centers, where she worked with founder and CEO Larry Wilson to design and implement change programs in large companies.

She lives outside Boston, Massachusetts, with her husband, George Daley, and their two sons.

Index

Learning from failure, 173, 189–201.
See also learning fast
developing approach for, 47–49
leader's responsibility for, 45, 47–58
orientation for, 47–48
psychological safety and, 99–100
responses for, 48–49
strategies for, 49–54
Learning orientation, 133
Lijek, Cora, 158–159
Lijek, Martin, 158–159
Limits, acknowledging, 165

M

McLuhan, Marshall, 59
Manufacturing Performance Institute
(MPI), 22
Marsalis, Wynton, 36
Mass production, 15–17
Meaning, 70–71, 150–155
Medical errors, 82–86, 151–154
Mendez, Tony, 159–161
Mental models, *see* Frames
Merchant, Nilofer, 79
Metaphors, 100–101
Metcalfe, Janet, 167
Mischel, Walter, 167
Mistakes, *see* Errors
Morath, Judith, 151–155
Motorola RAZR, 32–34, 101, 192, 193
MPI (Manufacturing Performance
Institute), 22
Mulally, Allan, 52
Mutual curiosity, 164–165

N

Naive realism, 39, 131
NASA, 19, 89–90
Negative, being, 94
Nembhard, Ingrid, 130
Netflix, 191
90-Day Plan:
benchmark goals, vii–viii, 1, 8–9,
75–76, 143–144, 205–206
performance goals, vii, 1, 7, 75,
143, 205

personal goals, viii, 9, 76, 144, 206
vision for success, viii, 9, 76, 144, 206
week by week guide to, 2–5

O

Occupational boundaries, 45–46, 65,
69–72, 163
Organizational change, 34, 105
Organizational culture, 95–96, 102,
131, 142
Organization-based boundaries, 65,
68–69, 71–72, 163
Organization man, 18
Organizing to execute, 14–15, 23–24
Organizing to learn, 22–24, 189–190
Outcome, process and, 133–134

P

Pahlavi, Mohammad Reza, 158
Participation, inviting:
at fearless organizations, 129–132, 165
by leaders, 98–99
with proactive inquiry, 131–132
with situational humility, 129–130
structures for, 132
Performance, organizational, 34, 85, 95
Performance goals, vii, 1, 7, 75, 143, 205
Performance situations, framing, 107–108
Personal goals, viii, 9, 76, 144, 206
Perturbations, 20
Physical distance, as boundary, 61, 62,
65, 66, 162
Pilot projects, 182–185
Pixar, 194
Post-it Notes, 100
Practice sessions, for learning frame, 117
Preventable failures, 50, 53
Prevention orientation, 108
Proactive inquiry, 124, 131–132
Problems, talking about, 153–154
Process:
guidelines for, 166
inadequate, 175, 177, 183
outcome and, 133–134
Product development teams, 63–64,
68–70, 162–163

215

Index

OTHER BOOKS IN THE
90 DAYS SERIES

90 Days to Level Up • ISBN: 978-1-394-25796-6

90 Days to Level Up • ISBN: 978-1-394-25793-5